AF488348

FINDING PIXEL DUST

STORIES AND REFLECTIONS FOR BUILDING
A MEANINGFUL CREATIVE CAREER

E.H. DE LA ESPRIELLA

FINDING PIXEL DUST
Stories and Reflections for Building a Meaningful Creative Career

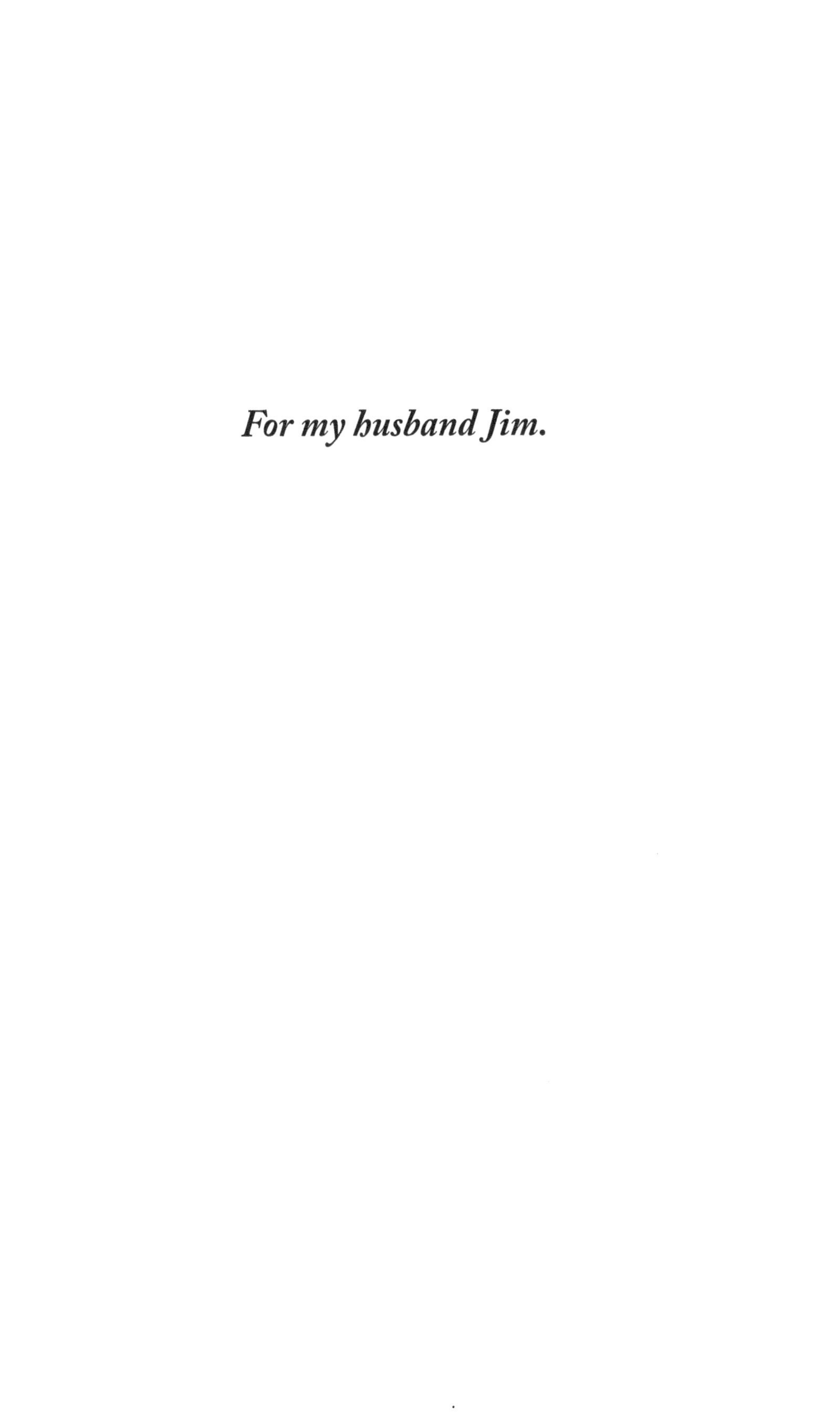

For my husband Jim.

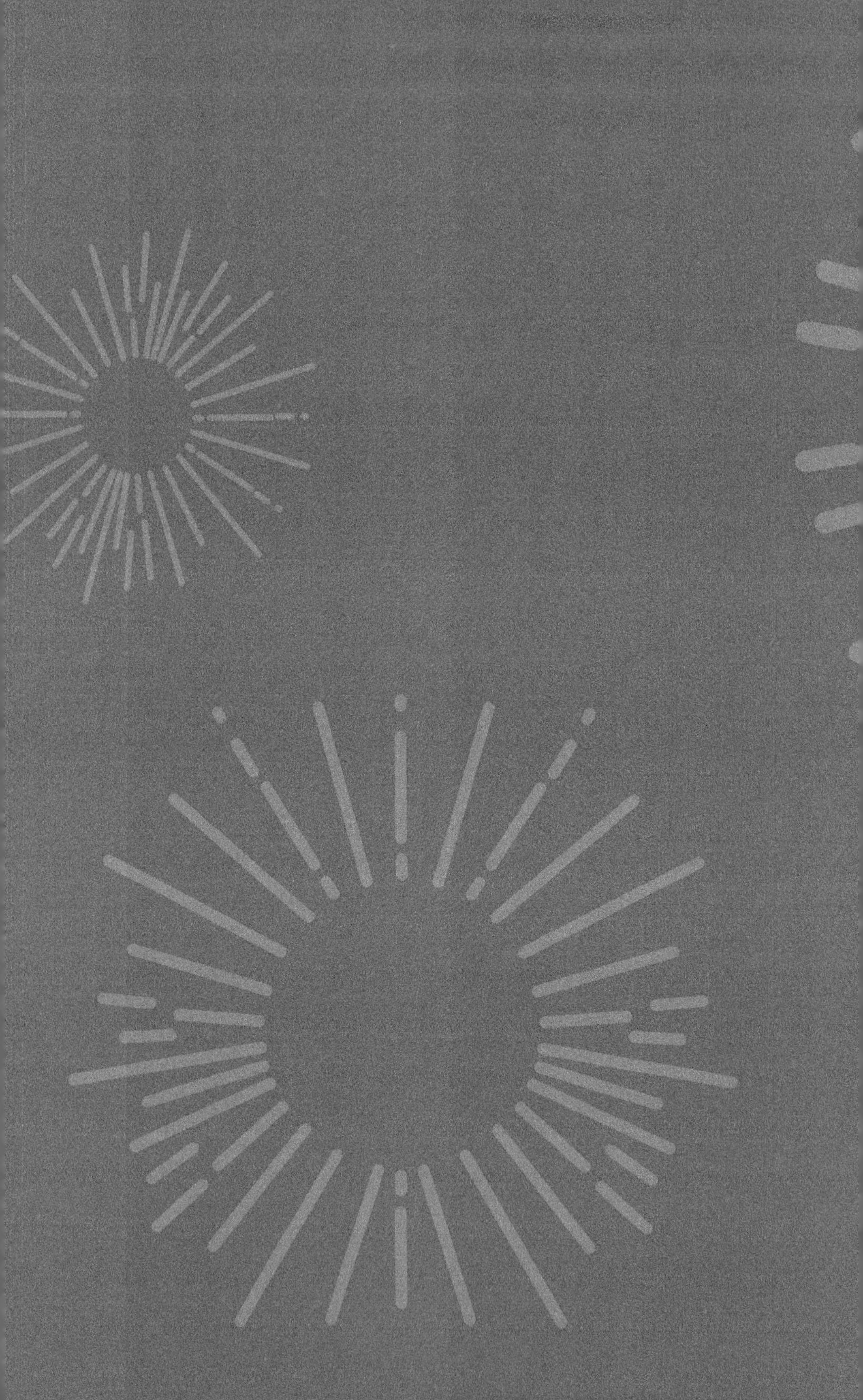

FINDING PIXEL DUST

PART ONE

WHY I WROTE THIS BOOK

This is the story of a career in graphic design, how I got to where I am today and the many challenges that shaped me along the way. I wrote the book I wish I had read when I was starting out.

Back then, over 35 years ago, there were plenty of self-help books, but not many that spoke directly to artists or graphic designers. This book is for artists, and really, for anyone in a creative career.

Part biography and part guide, this book is filled with those lessons I gathered through childhood, education, and work. It's about how I stumbled into the world of design, mostly by accident, or maybe just by being in the right place at the right time, and how I managed to leave a mark through the work I created and the creativity I brought to each role.

My goal is to answer some of the questions I had when I was younger and unsure (and scared) of which path to take. I want to set realistic expectations for what it's like to work in a creative field, and hopefully, inspire you to find your place in it too. If I made it, you can too.

WHAT DO YOU WANT TO DO WHEN YOU GROW UP?

When I was a kid, I wanted to be a doctor. I was fascinated by anatomy, how the body worked, how all the internal parts connected. One Christmas, I asked for Gray's Anatomy, the detailed medical text, and I studied its pages even though many of the terms were far beyond my understanding.

During those years, my uncle Carlitos was studying dentistry. I remember him sharing what he was learning, and while I found it interesting, the clinical side, the blood, the surgeries, the dissection, quickly made me realize that medicine wasn't for me. I respect those who can do that work, but I knew I wasn't cut out for it. I certainly didn't have the passion as my uncle did.

Then came another dream: my brother and I would build a marionette theater. Not just any theater, a lavish space inspired by the Paris Opera House, complete with three picturesque stages and silk-costumed puppets. Our opening production would be *Sleeping Beauty*, of course. That childhood fantasy still lingers in my mind. I sometimes wonder what life would've been like had I followed that dream.

Later, I wanted to be a singer, thanks to Donny and Marie Osmond, and then a classical music composer because I used to compose entire symphonic movements in my head. Even today, they return to me sometimes. I never learned to read music, but I had a good ear. I could replicate melodies after hearing them once. That's how I ended up playing the baritone saxophone, and later the French horn in high school band.

Eventually, I dreamed of being an actor and a director. As a child, it was easy to get lost in make-believe, but I also began imagining the full productions, sets, costumes, even budgets. It wasn't just play anymore. It was vision.

I HATE MATH

Despite my passion for art and creativity, I felt internal and cultural pressure to pursue a more "practical" career, especially as I reached my senior year of high school. That's when computer classes were introduced into the curriculum for the first time. I was fascinated by what computers could do, so I set my sights on a degree in computer science.

I took several aptitude tests before graduating, and guess what? Computer science didn't show up anywhere in the results, but creativity results scored incredibly high. But I ignored the warning signs. My grades echoed the tests, I was barely scraping by in math, while excelling in creative and science-based classes. Still, I defied logic (literally) and enrolled in university to study computer science and statistics.

And my university experience was a disaster. I failed math classes one after another. And when you fail that hard, it changes you. I felt like a failure, not just in school, but in life. I compared myself to everyone else. Why was it so easy for them and so hard for me? That uncertainty lasted for years. I had no idea what to do with my life.

Adulthood hit hard after high school. I thought I'd walk right into success. Instead, I faced rejection and confusion. Was it fate? Was it my own poor decision-making? Or was it all just an accident? Eventually, I found design, or maybe design found me. I'll tell you how that happened in the next chapters. But before we get there, I need to tell you one more thing. When I was about six or seven years old, my brother and I went to see Disney's *Pinocchio*. That film marked me forever. The characters, the music, the animation, it transported me. I was completely lost in Pinocchio's world. I couldn't sleep for nights afterward, terrified that Monstro the whale would swallow my brother and me. I didn't know how movies like that were made. But I knew, deep down, I wanted to do that, whatever it was.

FINDING MY WAY

Despite my passion for art and creativity, I felt internal and cultural pressure to pursue a more "practical" career, especially as I reached my senior year of high school. That's when computer classes were introduced into the curriculum for the first time. I was fascinated by what computers could do, so I set my sights on a degree in computer science.

I took several aptitude tests before graduating, and guess what? Computer science didn't show up anywhere in the results, but creativity results scored incredibly high. But I ignored the warning signs. My grades echoed the tests, I was barely scraping by in math, while excelling in creative and science-based classes. Still, I defied logic (literally) and enrolled in university to study computer science and statistics.

And my university experience was a disaster. I failed math classes one after another. And when you fail that hard, it changes you. I felt like a failure, not just in school, but in life. I compared myself to everyone else. Why was it so easy for them and so hard for me? That uncertainty lasted for years. I had no idea what to do with my life.

Adulthood hit hard after high school. I thought I'd walk right into success. Instead, I faced rejection and confusion. Was it fate? Was it my own poor decision-making? Or was it all just an accident? Eventually, I found design, or maybe design found me. I'll tell you how that happened in the next chapters. But before we get there, I need to tell you one more thing. When I was about six or seven years old, my brother and I went to see Disney's *Pinocchio*. That film marked me forever. The characters, the music, the animation, it transported me. I was completely lost in Pinocchio's world. I couldn't sleep for nights afterward, terrified that Monstro the whale would swallow my brother and me. I didn't know how movies like that were made. But I knew, deep down, I wanted to do that, whatever it was.

GROWING UP IN PANAMA

Growing up in Panama, our family was soundly middle-class, but I never felt like I lacked anything. My father led government-managed hospital laundry facilities, and my mother, determined to earn her own income against my dad's wishes, became an English teacher at one of the country's most respected bilingual schools, a career she held for over 50 years.

Both of my parents had artistic talents they never formally pursued. They could draw beautifully, and I absorbed early techniques from them that still live in my work today. My mother was, and still is, a natural creative. She painted on porcelain, crafted ceramics, and brought magic into our lives. I'll never forget the time she painted the Disney Fab Five characters on our bedroom closet doors. It felt like living inside a dream.

In January 1976, our family took our first airplane trip to visit relatives in Chicago. We saw snow for the first time and built a snowman, pure joy. Our aunt and uncle took us to the Museum of Science and Industry and we got to see mummies and preserved animals we've had never seen before in person. That trip marked our first real glimpse of the world beyond Panama. Later that year, we visited Miami Beach and Disney near Orlando. It was unforgettable. Disney's celebration of the U.S. Bicentennial was dazzling. Seeing Mickey and Minnie in person was creatively electrifying for us as children. It felt like our imaginations had come alive. The Magic Kingdom was so vast we explored it over three full days, and my mom made sure we didn't miss a single attraction.

That vacation, along with the movies and TV shows we loved growing up, left a lasting creative imprint. I learned to draw Goofy, and one of my drawings was even published in a local newspaper. Drawing became a joyful pastime, especially when I could sit beside my parents, paper and pencil in hand, soaking up every moment.

BECOMING BILINGUAL AND SPREADING MY WINGS

My mother had a vision: her children would learn English early. Having both parents fluent in a second language gave us a strong foundation. She had studied with English-speaking nuns at an all-girls Catholic school and instilled the same discipline in us. Though she taught at our school, she made sure never to teach us directly, avoiding any perception of favoritism. I'm grateful for that foresight.

Our school was one of the country's oldest bilingual institutions, and in my final three years, I specialized in science. It was a challenging path, especially since math was never my strength as I described earlier, but I made it through thanks to the support of friends. We lifted each other up, determined not to leave anyone behind. (Yes, *Lilo and Stitch*'s "Ohana" now resonates for a reason.)

Before senior year, my mother gave me a gift that would shape my life: a 30-day bus tour across Europe with 14 other teens. She paid for it entirely on her own, saving every penny she had. At the time, I didn't grasp the magnitude of her sacrifice, but I would come to see that this was her way of planting a seed, showing me that dreams begin with intention and are grown with effort.

That journey changed me. I stood in front of iconic landmarks and historic art, tasted foods I'd never eaten, got tipsy on wine for the first time in my life, and experienced independence in a way that introduced me to myself. I was learning who I was outside the context of my family, outside Panama. I was beginning to sprout.

A DREAM DELAYED

Graduating high school was a hard-won victory and gave me hope for the future. I began researching universities in the U.S., drawn to the Art Institute of Chicago. With family nearby, I thought I might live with them while attending school. But every time I brought up the topic of studying abroad, my parents remained quiet. Supportive in theory, but silent in action.

One evening, my mother came into my room as I studied for a test and sat beside me on the bed. Her expression was heavy, and I knew something was wrong. I had no idea how this conversation would change my life. She gently told me the truth, they simply couldn't afford to send me to school overseas. That moment broke something in me. It felt like the future I'd worked for had just vanished. I could see the shame in her eyes. She had to say it alone. My father had withdrawn from family life after my brother's death and left her to carry the weight.

We discussed local options, but none matched my creative aspirations. I knew I wanted to study art, but I didn't know how, or if, that would ever be possible. I was insecure and easily swayed, caught in a cultural current that pushed me away from my instincts. I longed to belong. I wanted to succeed, but no one could define what success really meant.

I had no rich uncles, no scholarships, and no grants to help. So, I started saving from my first job. After a difficult conversation with my father, he agreed to help pay part of the fees to attend a private university in Panama. I chose computer science as my field of study, but it didn't stick. Four years of poor grades confirmed it wasn't my path.

ESCAPE AND AWAKENING

By 1989, Panama's political climate was collapsing under the weight of Noriega's dictatorship. Working for the U.S. Army at the time, I faced restrictions just for being employed by the American government. Just for that reason alone, my driver's license was suspended, and I couldn't legally leave the country. Life became dangerous and my personal safety upsetting.

In April, I was able to travel to Miami to stay with an aunt until things in Panama settled down. That December, just before Christmas, the U.S. launched a military invasion to oust Noriega. I woke up to my aunt shaking me in the middle of the night, telling me to go to her room to watch the news. Still half-asleep, I stood in her doorway as CNN showed images of helicopters flying into Panama City. Chaos. Destruction. Bodies in the streets.

And then everything went black. I had fainted, overcome by the shock. My aunt and cousin helped me regain consciousness, and I called home again and again until I finally got through. My family was safe. My mother described the explosions and the fear, but they had survived. And within days, Noriega was captured, and freedom was restored.

That moment taught me something no classroom or tour could. The weight of reality, the way trauma imprints on the soul, can't be explained. It has to be lived. And surviving it, just like surviving the grief of my brother's passing or the disappointment I was to my father, becomes a chapter in your becoming.

FIGHT OR FLIGHT

Studying computer science turned out to be an accidental strategic choice, though I didn't realize it at the time. Who would have thought that computers would become essential not only in technology, but in the creative fields too, including design and animation?

After relocating to Miami, I began working at Royal Caribbean Cruises corporate offices. Even though it was not what I wanted to do at the time, it was just a new beginning. The job helped me expand my network, and more importantly, it introduced me to a much-needed circle of friends. I already had one close friend in Miami, Judy, who became a source of strength during a period of profound culture shock.

It doesn't matter where you're from or where you go, changing your surroundings is disorienting. I eventually learned how normal it was to feel lost for a while. Judy and I would escape into the night, hitting the clubs in Miami and Miami Beach, and I got to meet a lot of new people through her. She kept me grounded when everything felt uncertain. She gave me hope when I wanted to return home because of how disconnected I felt with life in general. At that time, staying in touch with my family in Panama was difficult and expensive, there were no smartphones or free text messaging apps. Being far from home felt truly far.

Having a background in computers got me the job at the cruise line, and that's where I began to build my first true network in the U.S. outside of my friend Judy's support circle. While I enjoyed the stability, I still felt adrift. I drew in the evenings, more as therapy than intention. I didn't really have a plan, I was just trying to get through each day. I was growing up in real time, on my own, paying rent, handling bills, and working full-time. Some days I enjoyed my work, but often I caught myself wondering what else might be out there. I knew I didn't want to work for the cruise industry and in sales for the rest of my life.

At the time, the cruise line was growing fast, adding new ships to their fleet and climbing the industry ranks.

I managed to transfer to other departments and meet people across different levels of the company.

One afternoon, while on a break in the company's garden overlooking Biscayne Bay and downtown Miami, a new colleague struck up a conversation. His name was Roger. He had recently started as an Account Executive, and for reasons I couldn't explain, he seemed drawn to me. Maybe it was my quiet demeanor, or the restlessness I was carrying so openly.

We hit it off, became close friends, and started hanging out after work. In our conversations, the subject of dreams came up. Roger asked me what I really wanted to do with my life, and for the first time in my life, I said it out loud: "I want to be an animator." It almost felt like I was speaking a different language or as if I was someone else. I couldn't believe how frank I was. And then he asked me a simple but life-altering question:

"If that's what you want, what's holding you back?"

That question stuck with me. I realized that the biggest thing holding me back … was me. I had been living under a cloud of self-doubt for so long that I'd stopped giving myself any credit. It took a stranger, now a friend, to point out what I couldn't see: I was the one standing in my own way because of lack of planning and knowledge that I owned my own possibilities.

Around this time, Disney had just opened its third theme park in Orlando, Disney-MGM Studios, and I'd visited not long before. Seeing professional animators working behind glass during the park's animation tour lit something inside me. I even caught a glimpse of Ruben A. Aquino, a legendary Disney animator. That same year, *The Lion King* hit theaters. I still remember watching that opening sequence with friends, chills running through my spine. It was magic. It brought me back to the feeling I had as a child watching *Pinocchio* and *Sleeping Beauty*. I'd fallen under the Disney spell again. But I was in Miami, feeling like a nobody, stuck, unsure, and completely lost.

Can you relate?

Roger's support sparked a shift. I began to form a loose plan. With growing confidence, I applied to New World School of the Arts, a program within Miami Dade Community College. I assembled a portfolio of drawings, paintings, and collages, and was surprisingly accepted. Surprised because I didn't know I had it in me, but here I was doing it. First step: done.

I fell in love with this new path of creative education.

I took figure drawing classes multiple times just to master the skill Disney animation required. For maybe the second time in my life, I felt like I was exactly where I belonged, doing something I absolutely loved.

Drawing became my focus. Slowly, my portfolio grew. For the first time, I was building a foundation for the raw creative energy I had always carried inside. Before, I had been designing and drawing without a true sense of structure or purpose. New World School of the Arts gave me the fundamentals I was missing.

Art History class in particular changed everything. Learning about Egyptian and Chinese aesthetics opened my eyes to style, meaning, and intention. I began seeing my work through a broader lens, understanding not just how to create, but why. Being naturally inquisitive helped me dive into those historical contexts, and it's a trait that continues to inform my creative process today. Every artist needs a foundation. Mine began here.

Ask Yourself:

- Do you enjoy learning about other cultures, especially the reasons behind their art and design?
- Do you see visual ideas in everyday life, colors,

textures, patterns, even music, or movement, swirling in your imagination?

- Do you find yourself daydreaming about creative projects, films, symphonies, stories, even surreal dreams, mapping them out in your head?
- When you make art, does it come naturally to you, or do you struggle?
- When you do struggle, do you look for help to overcome it?
- Do you have a circle of support, friends, family, teachers, or mentors, who give you honest, helpful feedback?

These are the kinds of questions I began asking myself as I stepped deeper into my artistic path. One day at work, I was talking with my supervisor about my hopes and dreams. I shared how badly I wanted to pursue something creative, maybe even work for Disney one day. She already knew I was studying at the art school and she'd often see me sketching during my breaks. At that point, I was drawing all the time.

What she said next surprised me: she told me about a former employee who had once worked at our company but had since moved to work for Disney Animation. She offered to connect us. It felt like I had just won the lottery.

Of course, nothing had actually happened yet, but the possibility lit me up. After work that same day, I called Roger to share the news. I didn't know if this woman would answer my call, let alone take an interest in helping me. All we had in common was a shared employer, past and present.

But to my surprise, she called me back. She told me her story, which mirrored mine more than I expected, she too had lived in Miami, had gone to art school, and pursued her dreams in Orlando. She offered to meet the next time she came to visit her family. A month later, during the holidays in 1993, she came to my apartment and reviewed my drawings.

To be honest, I didn't have much, mostly figure drawing sketches from class. I could tell she wasn't overly impressed, but she was kind, generous with her feedback, and clear about what I needed to work on.

Here are some of the key lessons she shared with me, wisdom I want to pass on:

1. One weak piece can ruin an entire portfolio. Every sample you include should be strong and consistent.

2. Life drawings and gesture sketches are essential. Show that you understand how the human body moves, this applies to animals and inanimate objects, too.

3. Stylized drawings need strong foundations. Your exaggerations and abstractions should still show that you understand structure.

4. Dimensionality matters. Make figures or effects pop off the page, create the illusion of depth and motion.

5. A solid portfolio contains 10–20 varied pieces. Not too many, not too few, and each should serve a purpose.

That meeting changed me. I came away not just with feedback, but with a renewed sense of direction. She didn't tear me down. Instead, she focused on what was possible. She saw my potential and my passion, and that gave me fuel to keep going.

She also gave me practical next steps. She told me

about Disney's internship program, where to apply, and what kind of work would be expected. Her visit, her kindness, and her belief in me sparked something I hadn't felt in a long time, ambition.

I began drawing more than ever. Every day. But deep down, I knew my work still wasn't ready. Some of her comments stayed with me, feeding the insecure voice in my head. But this time, that voice didn't win. I used it as motivation. I knew I could get better, and I did.

Eventually, I put together a stronger portfolio and submitted it to Disney Feature Animation for their next internship round. She had warned me: Disney receives thousands of submissions every year, and the competition is fierce. Passion alone wouldn't be enough, my work had to stand out.

A few months later, the envelope arrived with an answer. A real envelope, from Disney. I held it like it was treasure, my hands shaking. I hadn't even opened it yet, but the very act of receiving it filled me with possibility. I had done something. I had taken a risk. I had moved closer to my dream.

I opened the envelope slowly, reading every word. They thanked me for my submission but informed me that I wasn't selected. The reason? My samples didn't show enough detail in figures-in-motion, an essential quality for animation. And they were right. That had always been a weakness in my work. I could draw static figures, but I struggled to give them that sense of life, that animated energy Disney required.

I was crushed. I felt defeated, like maybe I had been fooling myself all along. Maybe I wasn't ready. Maybe I wasn't good enough. My contact had warned me how hard this would be, and she was right. Still, it hurt. Bad.

But rejection is part of the journey. I wasn't done yet.

MANAGING DEFEAT AND REJECTION

Receiving that rejection letter from Disney hit me harder than I ever expected. I felt gutted. All the encouragement I'd received from friends, teachers, and mentors suddenly rang hollow. Everyone had told me I had talent. Everyone had said, "You should apply." And now here I was, with my dream denied. Now I understood how my friend must have felt when she got rejected for a part in *Hello Dolly!* But I didn't take it out on anyone.

For months, I spiraled into a deep depression. The rejection shook something in me, not just creatively, but personally. I questioned everything, my talent, my potential, my purpose. Nights were spent staring at the ceiling, wondering if working at a cruise line was all I was ever meant to do. It felt like the world was telling me:

"This is it. Settle."

But deep down, I knew it wasn't my *ikigai*—my reason for being. I had more to give. I wanted to give more. This was NOT my purpose in life. And slowly, very slowly, I started to understand something: the fact that I had even tried meant I had already made it halfway up the hill. I couldn't stop now.

This realization didn't come overnight. It took weeks, then months, to crawl out of that low. I had to grieve the loss, not just of the opportunity, but of the fantasy I had built up around it. I'm a deeply sensitive person, and this rejection wasn't just professional, it was personal. That's how invested I was.

And I want to say this clearly: I don't regret how hard I took it. Some people bounce back quickly. Others give up entirely. But for people like me, those of us who feel everything, it's a process. We have to live through every stage of it: denial, anger, sadness, and eventually, acceptance, the hard way.

I learned that rejection is subjective. One reviewer might prefer a different style or technical strength. And in that subjectivity, there's room to grow, not to internalize failure, but to evolve. Once I was able to release the sadness and disappointment, I began to live again and I began to draw again.

My friends reminded me: "This was your first application. Most people don't get in the first time." They were right. At that time, traditional animation internships were scarce. Disney accepted only a handful of artists from around the world. I was competing against talent I couldn't even imagine, many with incredible talent and years of training behind them.

Six months later, I tried again. Another rejection. Then again. Rejected a third time.

Each denial brought a wave of emotional collapse, periods of depression that started to affect my personal life in new, unsettling ways. I questioned whether I'd ever be good enough. I wondered if I'd ever make it as an animator, or if Disney was just a dream I needed to let go of.

But something kept me going. Maybe it was the fact that other people worked there, too. Real people, like me. Maybe it was the voice of my Disney contact, still encouraging me to keep trying. She told me something I've never forgotten:

"This isn't failure. It's a step closer to success. Now you

know what not to do. Use it."

That simple reframing helped me reclaim part of myself. It gave me back a sense of identity I had lost in the rejection.

At work, I became more restless. The cruise line job, once a source of stability, now felt like a box I couldn't breathe in. My dream still hovered on the horizon, and I couldn't ignore it anymore.

I had no safety net, no promises, no job offers. But I had a desire to move forward. My friends kept me afloat emotionally, but I was on my own in every other sense. There were nights I cried myself to sleep, questioning everything. But the flame never went out.

By summer 1994, I made a bold decision: I would move to Orlando with no job lined up and just three months' worth of savings. I packed my things and said goodbye to Miami, the city that had been both a home and a crucible.

Leaving was bittersweet. I had met great people, but I had also endured some of the loneliest years of my life. I arrived in Miami as a shallow, aloof version of myself. I left as someone who had grown, struggled, and begun to understand the shape of his own resilience.

I owe much of that to my friend Judy. She and I had known each other since childhood in Panama. She moved to the States before I did, and we reconnected in Miami. She was my rock. When things got really bad, I'd crash at her apartment. We didn't have much, some nights, dinner was just spaghetti with cut-up hot dogs. But to us, it was a feast. Judy never gave up. She worked hard, pursued her dreams, and pushed through every obstacle with grit and grace. Watching her made me believe I could do the same.

We talked often about our goals and what we wanted to become. She was resilient in a way I admired deeply. Stronger than I was. But she never made me feel small. She lifted me up.

Living in Miami taught me that life wasn't easy. There's no map. No guarantees. I was in a country I barely understood, trying to build a future from scratch. I had been in bad relationships that left me emotionally drained. By the time I left Miami, I had just come out of a rocky two-year relationship, another weight I carried with me to Orlando. But despite all of it, despite the rejections, the heartbreak, the self-doubt, I kept going. Because deep down, I still believed.

STARTING AGAIN

Arriving in Orlando felt like I was taking my first real breath. It was a chance to start fresh, but the weight of not having a job still lingered. I told myself this move had to mean something. I made a quiet promise: I would find the job of my dreams, and maybe, just maybe, meet someone to share my life with. That emptiness I felt inside needed filling.

That first week, I drove to the Disney Casting Center in Lake Buena Vista. The building was like something out of Alice in Wonderland, with colorful murals leading into a whimsical lobby. I applied for anything they were hiring for, but one role stood out: resort reservations. With my cruise line background, it seemed like an easy fit. It wasn't my dream job, but it was a foot in the door.

I interviewed that same day and left feeling hopeful. Then ... nothing. A week passed. Then two. Then three.

I started to worry. But about a month later, I got the call: I'd been hired as a temporary reservation sales agent starting in October. It was minimum wage, and there were no guarantees, but it was Disney. That call meant everything. What was even more appealing is that I would make a whopping 25 cents more because I spoke a second language.

Three weeks into training, something unexpected happened: our group was offered permanent positions. I officially had a job, and with it, the door to possibility cracked open a little wider.

Six months in, I met with my supervisor to talk about growth opportunities. I shared that I hoped to one day work in feature animation since I loved anything creative and I was good in drawing. Her response took me by surprise.

She looked at me and said, "You just started here. And honestly, do you really think you have what it takes?" She didn't know me at all. She'd never seen my art. But somehow, she felt entitled to shut down my dream. Was it because I was young? Because I was Latino? Because I spoke one more language than she did? Her words stung. But they also lit a fire. I walked away from her sad little office determined to prove her wrong. From that moment on, I focused all my energy on finding a way out of the reservation department.

Still, a year and a half later, I was answering phones. There were days when I felt I would never escape. The ache to be an artist never left me, it only grew stronger.

One bright spot came when I helped train new hires. One of the new cast members told me her brother was a special effects animator at the studio. She introduced us, and through him, I started building connections.

One afternoon, I met with a lead animator from *The Lion King* at a nearby restaurant. He brought a colleague with him. Both looked through my portfolio and offered kind, constructive feedback. By that point, my work had improved significantly, but the industry was changing fast. Traditional animation was slowly being replaced by digital techniques, and they were now struggling what to make of their own careers.

I kept applying for every creative opening I could find. Back then, the job listings came out every Thursday, printed, posted in binders, old school. I kept applying every week. And with patience, something changed.

In 1996, I got a call. It was for a new position at the

Studio, a role in the updated animation tour where artists would draw characters live for park guests. I had applied for the internship program nine times by now and never got past the portfolio stage. But now, they wanted to interview me.

I submitted my updated work, went through multiple interviews, and waited.

Weeks passed. The anxiety crept in, familiar and unwelcome. I braced for rejection, it was evident that by now, they had decided to go with someone else. But I was wrong. I got the call. I had been selected. Though, the job was temporary, just for the summer. After that, I'd have to go back to reservations. But this time, it was different. I had a foot inside the animation building. There was no going back, not emotionally, not spiritually. I had finally touched the dream.

The role involved presenting to audiences in the new guided Studio tour. We had to draw live on camera while triggering video cues and lighting effects, and eventually reveal a view of the animation studio behind a frosted glass panel.

We launched the new show alongside the release of *The Hunchback of Notre Dame*. I had to learn to draw the characters quickly and accurately, while performing in front of an audience. I hadn't been on stage in years, so my first show was nerve-racking, I had to remember every cue, every button, every line of the script. But it was magic. I was finally working as an artist, for Disney!

As the end of the assignment approached, something unexpected happened. My new supervisor from the reservation center mentioned that his wife managed the animation gallery store, the place guests visited after walking out of the tour. She'd seen my show and was looking for an artist to paint animation cels "on stage."

I asked if I could meet her, so he set it up. I applied through the appropriate channel, interviewed, and auditioned. They needed to see if I could paint a cel with the precision required. Luckily, I had been practicing the painting process with cel kits sold in the gallery store. I passed the test easily.

When my animation tour role ended, I transitioned directly into Ink & Paint, and I never returned to the reservation center again.

LIFE BEHIND THE GLASS

The Ink & Paint job was intense. We had daily quotas and painted in full view of guests behind a glass partition we called "The Fishbowl." Although cel painting for feature films had gone digital by this time, we continued preserving the tradition by producing artwork for the collectible market.

There was variety, too: we painted, mixed colors by hand to match the color models, restocked inventory, and often worked directly with guests to explain the process. In addition to my regular work in Ink and Paint, I had some incredible opportunities to exercise my drawing abilities with a couple of side projects. First came The Animation Celebration (1996) at the Disney-MGM Studios: A Hunchback mall tour event with cutting-edge tech, though sweltering summer heat made it less magical. But I was able to take advantage of my onstage past experiences and creative talent.

A year later, I had yet another opportunity to work in the Hercules Mega Mall Tour (1997). I auditioned over video conference (a new thing back then) and had to draw Mickey Mouse while answering questions from the show director. Thanks to my animation tour experience, I nailed it. I was selected as an understudy for the tour and trained in California for 30 days that January, meeting animators like Nik Ranieri and Eric Goldberg. We practiced drawing *Hercules* characters under tight time constraints and rehearsed stage shows with a cast of incredibly talented performers, many of whom went on to become stars on Broadway and television. I personally toured 13 cities across the U.S. and Canada. I visited the Burbank studio. I saw kids light up when I sketched characters in real time. I got to do what I loved, and it felt like I was finally living my dream.

TIPPING POINTS AND TURNING PAGES

Eventually, things began to shift. Traditional animation was dying. Digital technology was taking over. Work felt more limited, and though I contributed creatively, designing a special *Mulan* cel with a watercolor background and edition stamp, it wasn't enough to satisfy the fire I had inside.

I applied to every possible role in feature animation, checker, in-betweener, effects, even for an entry level production assistant. I took an animation checker test and scored perfectly, caught every intentional error. The hiring manager, someone I knew, said it was the best test they'd ever seen. Still, I didn't get the job. They gave it to someone already in the department. It was crushing. Was I not good enough? Was it because I am Latino? Because I am gay? I don't know. But the silence said enough.

Then, in a way to feed my ambition, I began to look elsewhere for opportunities. DreamWorks and other studios in California and Vancouver, Canada were hiring for many positions in those days. I was especially drawn to DreamWorks at the time, they had just released *The Prince of Egypt*, which I had seen several times, completely mesmerized by how deeply moving it was. I started applying to anything and everything. I was obsessed.

One day, I received a response from DreamWorks. They were interested in having me test for an in-betweener position, an animator role responsible for drawing the frames that fill in the movements between the key drawings. It's tedious work, often uncredited, but it's how many animators get their foot in the door. This could be it, I thought. The break I was waiting for. The only caveat was that I needed to take the test in person at their studio.

After several emails with the animation recruiter, I nervously brought up the idea to my boyfriend (now husband): a trip to California to take the test. I knew it was a long shot. I had already been rejected from Disney so many times. But I couldn't shake the feeling that this mattered. My grandmother's voice echoed in my mind, her belief that we must take chances, or we'll never know what might have been. So, we booked a trip within our means, choosing a modest hotel near the DreamWorks campus in Glendale.

I'll never forget the moment he dropped me off at the studio that morning. The studio campus looked like a Spanish villa, beautiful, quiet, almost surreal. The recruiter met me and kindly gave me a short tour. I remember how peaceful it felt, how still. Eventually, I was brought to a small studio room with an animation desk prepped just for me. On it sat a test packet, pencils, erasers, and a note with instructions. I was to complete five frames.

When I opened the test folder, I gasped. The scene was from *The Prince of Egypt*, a close-up of Moses' face. I had to animate five drawings between the first and last key frames. Just five. But they had to be perfect.

The test lasted eight hours, and I was on cloud nine the entire time. I had done in-between work before, but this was different. This was the real thing. I obsessed over every line, every nuance, trying to demonstrate detail, control, understanding of movement. The irony, of course, is that those five drawings would go by in a blink on screen, barely even noticed by the audience. But without them, the scene wouldn't feel real at all.

When my boyfriend picked me up later in the afternoon, I was exhausted, emotionally and physically drained. I had given it everything. And despite my nerves, I truly felt I had done well.

Back home, I followed up with a heartfelt thank-you note to the recruiter, hopeful. A week passed. Nothing. I emailed again. Finally, I received a call. The recruiter told me I had done a good job. Just not quite good enough. I wasn't selected. But he encouraged me to keep applying.

Another rejection. Another heartbreak. But somehow, I still didn't stop believing.

During this difficult time, I kept building relationships throughout the local studio, hoping to stay inspired even when the door to feature animation remained closed. At that point, Disney Design Group was still housed in the same building as feature animation, which was a fortunate overlap. This was the department responsible for creating all the incredible merchandise, art, and collectibles sold

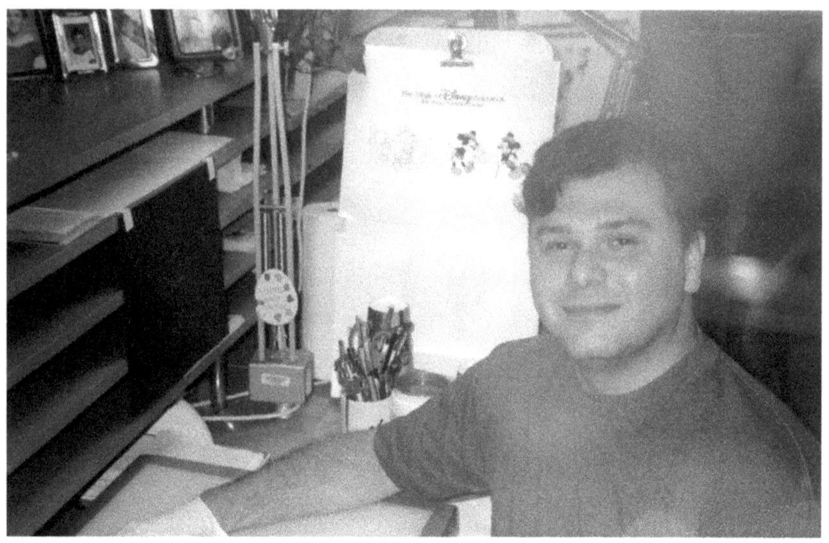

Working in the Fish Bowl in the Ink and Paint Department, 1996. ©Disney

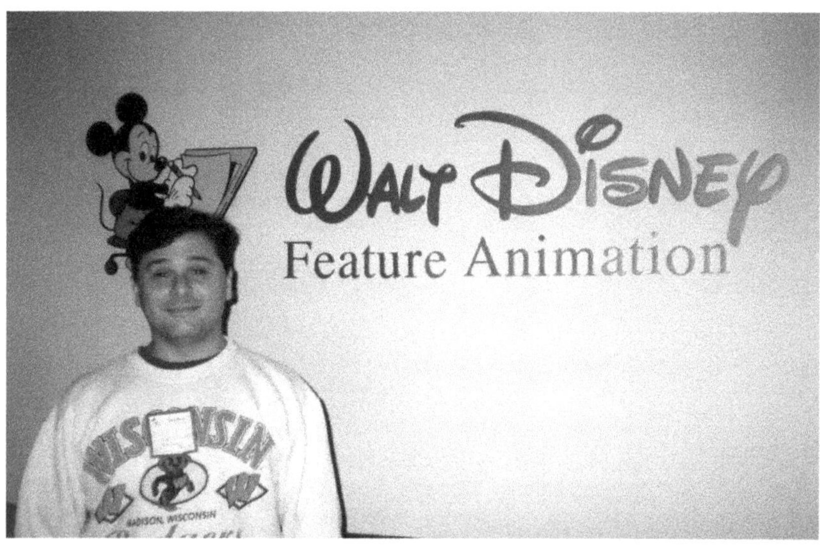

In the clouds at the Walt Disney Feature Animation building in Burbank while training for the *Disney's Hercules* Mega Mall Tour, January 1997. ©Disney

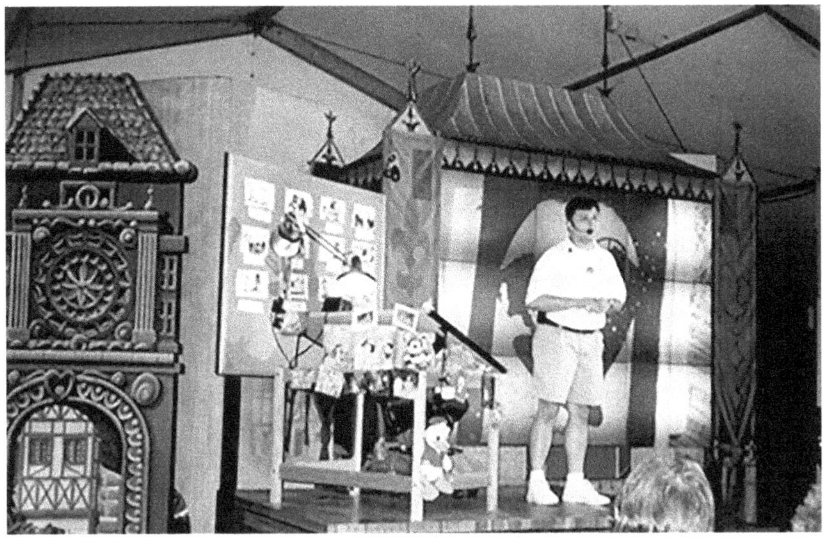

Performing in the *Disney's Hunchback of Notre Dame* Animation Celebration.
©Disney

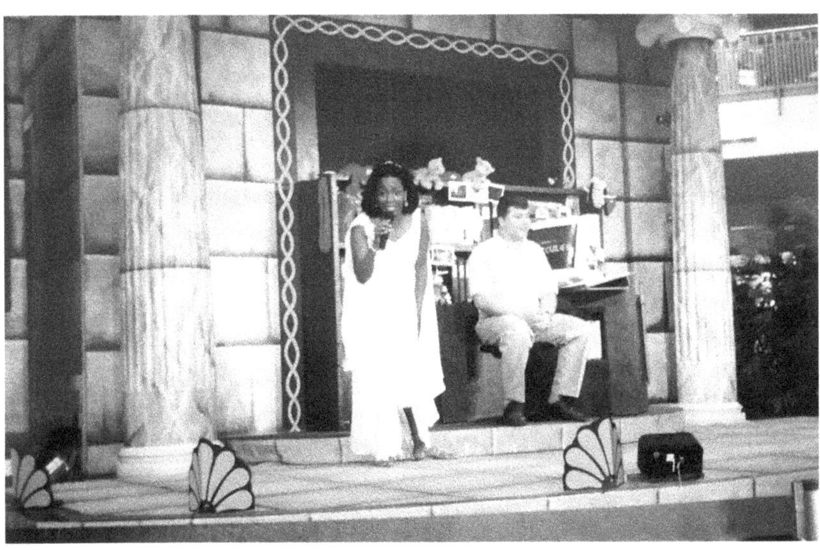

Performing with Connie Jackson at the *Disney's Hercules* Mega Mall Tour, 1997.
©Disney

at the parks and online, and among the many talented artists I had the privilege of meeting, I was especially lucky to cross paths with Ralph Kent.

Ralph was a creative leader with a remarkable history. He had played an instrumental role in maintaining the high standards required for Mickey Mouse artwork, ensuring the character's global appeal remained consistent and iconic. He was even credited with designing the first Mickey Mouse watch. But what truly struck me was that Ralph had a direct connection to Walt Disney himself, having worked at the Burbank studio during the golden era of animation. Meeting him felt surreal, I was both honored and humbled. He was a Disney legend in his own right, and somehow, here he was, talking to me.

Through my work in Ink and Paint, I gradually got to know him more, and one day I mustered the courage to ask if he would be willing to teach me a thing or two about his drawing techniques. To my surprise and deep gratitude, he said yes. He took the time to mentor me, offering advice on how to draw expressive, fluid lines, lines that conveyed weight, character, and emotion. Until then, I hadn't even considered the way a line could carry such depth. But Ralph had a way of revealing the soul of a drawing.

What meant the most to me wasn't just what he taught, it was how generous he was with his knowledge. He didn't treat me like someone in a low-level role; he treated me like an artist, like someone at his own level. He saw something in me or at least encouraged me to see it in myself. The moments I spent with him were more than educational, they were empowering. I felt like I belonged. He made me believe I could do it. Still, despite that progress and the connections I had made, I remained challenged in getting anywhere close to the roles I truly dreamed of. But those early encouragements, especially from someone like Ralph, were fuel. They kept me going.

Eventually, I asked myself the hardest question: Why am I fighting so hard to be part of something that doesn't want me? In the end, one day I called a hiring manager at the studio that I had been communicating with for some time to find out about any upcoming opportunities and she said something that shook me awake:

"Why are you still chasing feature animation? The whole department's falling apart."

And she was right. Not long after, Disney shut down

the Florida studio, laying off almost everyone.

That rejection, the one that stung the most, may have been the biggest blessing. But at the time, I couldn't see that. I only knew that I had tried with everything I had. That I had come far. And that maybe, just maybe, it was time to dream in a new direction.

GRAPHIC DESIGN: MY UNEXPECTED DESTINY

By the end of the 1990s, it became clear that computer animation was taking over. Traditional methods were fading, and with them, many of the roles I had once dreamed of. I had spent years chasing the goal of working in feature animation, but now the goalposts were moving, and I had no choice but to move with them.

I started looking for a new path. I had always had an eye for design and a deep love for art. Now the question became: how could I use those two things to build a new future? The truth was, I didn't have a plan. I never learned how to plan for the long term. I didn't grow up with that mindset, and I felt the consequences of it now.

But creativity had always pulled at me, even when I tried to pretend that I belonged somewhere else. As I told you in the beginning of the book, I thought that I wanted to be a doctor. It sounded like the right kind of impressive. But the truth? It didn't light me up. Art did. I kept coming back to it in every conversation, every daydream, every sketchbook. It fulfilled me. It made me feel whole.

Toward the end of my final year in Ink & Paint, around 2000, I found an online school that offered a certificate in graphic design. It is called sessions.edu, and the best part was that I could learn at my own pace. That mattered to me. I didn't feel rushed. I could go slow, absorb everything, and really get it.

At that time, Sessions only offered certificates, but today they offer full degrees. Back then, that certificate was exactly what I needed. I had the instinct for design, but I didn't have the foundation. I didn't know the "why" behind the things I created. I wanted to understand the rules so I could eventually break them with purpose.

I also started teaching myself Adobe programs like Photoshop and Illustrator. Back then, the software came in separate packages, each with its own instruction manual. I used the *Classroom in a Book* series to learn how to use them and made a promise to myself: two hours a night, every night after work. Just me, the computer, and a growing hunger to figure it out. And so, I began creating personal projects to build my portfolio, flyers, mock ads, posters, anything I could think of. I wasn't just going through the motions. I was slowly falling in love with design.

A year later, I earned my certificate in graphic design. It took time, but the more I studied, the more confident I became. I finally started to believe in my own talent, not because someone else told me I was good, but because I saw the evidence in my own work.

By then, I had already left the Ink & Paint department and taken a job at Disney Cruise Line's main offices. It was a step back, at least on paper. But emotionally and mentally, it was a step I desperately needed. Ink & Paint was becoming creatively stifling. I needed air from all the negativity happening in animation at that time and the creative limitations of the job.

The cruise line job wasn't glamorous, but it gave me something important: space. Space to heal, space to study, and unexpectedly, a space to create. And a way to start over. While working there, they needed posters and materials for internal events, especially around diversity and inclusion, which were starting to become a bigger part of the company's culture. I volunteered to help with my newly learned design skills. It gave me real design experience with real deadlines. More than that, it gave me purpose again.

During that transitional period, I also started painting in oils. I had no formal training, so I just picked up a canvas and started to paint like my life depended on it. And maybe, in a way, it did. Those years were hard and emotionally draining. There were days I felt lost all over again, but painting helped me stay grounded. The slowness of it, the layering of color, the waiting, it taught me patience. It gave me a safe place to put all the emotion I couldn't always speak out loud. Painting became a kind of therapy, and it gave me something to hold onto while I figured out where I was going next.

When I finally felt ready, I started applying for graphic design jobs. This time, I approached it differently. After so many rejections from feature animation, I had learned a thing or two about what it meant to be prepared, and about not tying my self-worth to every outcome.

By this point, designing had become second nature. I was doing it constantly, just for the love of it. I gave myself assignments and created without pressure. Somehow, that made everything easier.

Then, in 2001, I landed my first official graphic design job with the sales department. It all began with a panel interview of three people. I walked in carrying a printed copy of my portfolio, not just to show off my design work, but to demonstrate that I understood the full process: layout, production, and printing techniques that go beyond what's seen on screen. I could tell they were impressed, and within a week, I received an offer. It was a major milestone. No favors, no inside connections, just my work, my preparation, and my passion. It felt like my first real win in this new chapter of my life.

When I got the offer, I was stunned at the salary. I had never earned that much in my life. It felt surreal, like I had suddenly struck gold. My boyfriend and I went out to dinner that night, not just to celebrate the new job, but to honor what it truly represented: a turning point, a career launch, and a quiet validation that all the sacrifices were finally paying off. Coincidentally, we also celebrated my boyfriend's promotion, literally on the same day.

What's funny is that the sales department was housed in the reservation center building. Just knowing this gave me a rush of emotions, some good, many difficult. This is where my Disney career had started years before and where I met my husband. This is also where I met Shellie who was pivotal in connecting me to feature animation through her brother Tony. I was so traumatized by the work in reservations, I had this irrational fear that they might suddenly pull me back onto the phones if the company was short-staffed, which was something I knew deep down I could never do again.

That first day was unforgettable. My desk was in a small, shared office with three or four other employees, and waiting for me was a welcome box filled with swag, a gesture that instantly made me feel seen and appreciated. As the hours passed and I got to meet the team and my new leader, I felt something I hadn't in a long time. I felt like I belonged.

Looking back, I realize that I had been chasing animation for the wrong reasons. I didn't just want the job, I wanted that screen credit, the status and the validation. But would I have loved doing it every day?

Would it have fulfilled me? Probably not. It had just become an unhealthy obsession.

Graphic design was different. It wasn't about proving something. It was about expression and about problem-solving. It was about creating something beautiful and functional at the same time. I wasn't competing against anyone else anymore, just myself. That shift changed everything in me.

GETTING CREATIVE FEEDBACK IN THIS NEW WORLD OF DESIGN

In any job, we receive feedback, sometimes directly, but more often, indirectly. We're told to learn from it, grow from it, but no one ever really teaches us how to receive feedback. Or how to give it. They definitely didn't teach it in school, not in design school or in life. And yet, it's as vital a skill as managing money or understanding credit. If more people knew how to give and receive feedback constructively, the world, especially the world of design, would be a better place.

I learned this lesson early on during my first job in Sales. I had the privilege of working alongside another talented designer named John. We started around the same time, became close friends, and learned so much from each other. We shared our projects, swapped critiques, and always tried to uplift rather than tear down. We didn't even call it feedback, it was just how we worked. Honest, thoughtful, and kind. It was the best crash course in real-world design collaboration. That's where I began to understand that not all feedback is created equal.

There are two kinds of feedback: objective and subjective. Subjective feedback is personal opinion, "I don't like that color," or "Can we make it pop?" It's not based on design principles or communication goals. It's rooted in the person's individual preferences, their personal tastes, or even just their mood that day. Sometimes, it's downright random. I once had someone ask me to add a starburst to a layout, then later change it from blue to orange … just because. No reasoning or relevance, just because they saw something similar once and thought it worked. It happens a lot. Designers joke about this kind of feedback because it's often absurd, but the truth is, it can be exhausting. Still, sometimes, even the most subjective feedback hides a kernel of truth that can improve your work. You just have to know how to sift through the noise to find it.

Objective feedback, on the other hand, is rooted in design fundamentals. It's tied to clarity, hierarchy, color theory, typography, alignment, things that matter. It can also be rooted in the deep understanding of the intellectual message being conveyed and how it connects with the identity of the brand. When someone tells you a headline isn't readable or a layout feels off-balance, and they can explain why, that's gold. That's the kind of feedback that helps you grow.

But here's the challenge: most people don't speak the language of design. So as designers, it becomes part of our job to translate, to read between the lines, to understand the intent behind the comment, even if the words don't quite land right.

I've had people give me vague, one-line critiques that left me scratching my head, and others who offered feedback so detailed it left no room for creativity. In both cases, the trick is to build trust. Get to know the person giving the feedback and learn their style. Help them understand what kind of input is helpful to you. That's when the real collaboration starts.

When I get vague or overly subjective feedback, I respond with questions, not defensively, but out of curiosity. I ask:

"What's the reason behind that change? Did I miss something in the design brief?"

"Can you share more about what's not working for you so that I better understand the feedback?"

"What feeling are you hoping to evoke?"

I ask not because I want to challenge their opinion, but because I want to understand and offer a satisfying solution and get the project completed in time.

Sometimes I get asked to "move this image down a bit" or "make the headline bigger," and those little tweaks can unravel the entire structure of a design. That's why it's important to have a conversation.

The best way to avoid this kind of misalignment is to ask the right questions up front. When clients or leaders say, "Just play around with it," I cringe a little. It's like designing in the dark. It wastes time, energy, and creativity, and leads to disappointment for everyone.

But if they give me reference points, a phrase, an

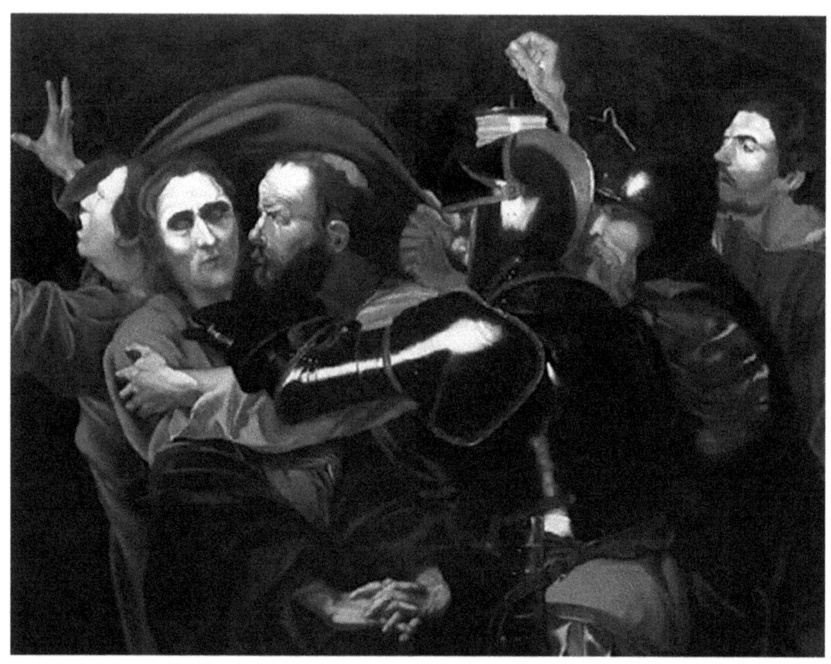

Study of Caravaggios's *The Taking of Christ*, oil on canvas, 60" x 48", 2001.

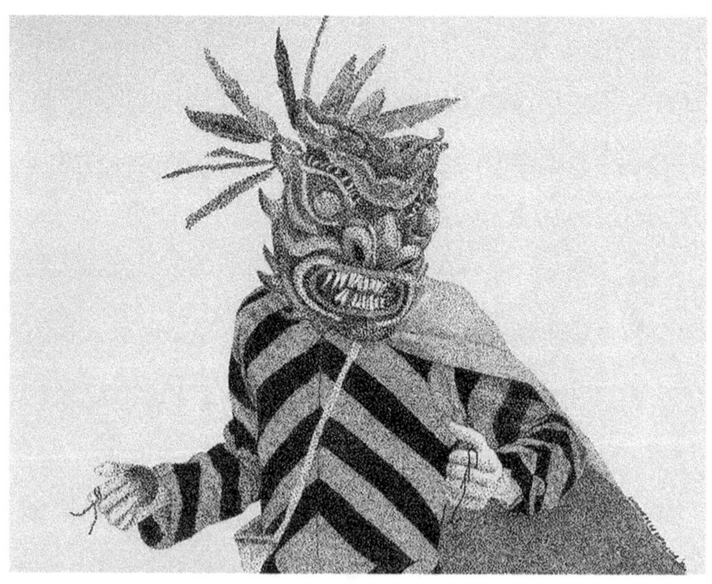

Diablico Sucio, ink pointillism on paper, 7" x 5"

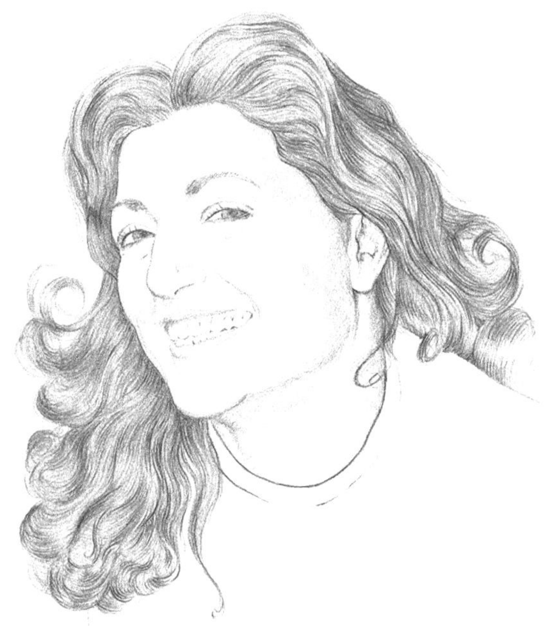

Zara, pencil on paper, 8" x 10", 2004.

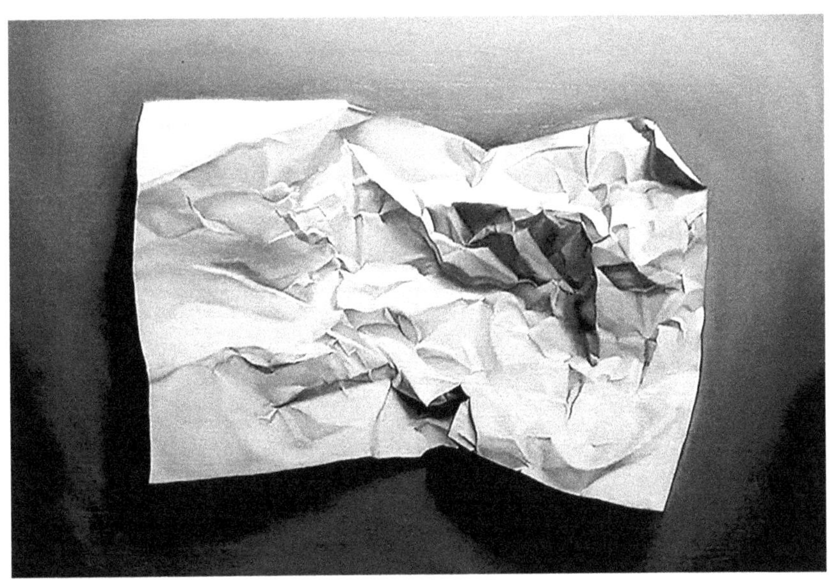

Unwrapped Nothing, oil on canvas, 18" x 12", 2007

explanation, a photo, a mood, even a scene from a film, I can build from that. Inspiration has many forms. Even poetry or sculpture can become a foundation for a strong design concept.

The truth is that many people don't know how to give design feedback. They don't have the vocabulary or the training. That's why working under a seasoned creative director or art director is such a gift. You can feel the difference in the feedback. It's structured and much more insightful, and respectful. It leaves room for your creativity while still challenging you to push your ideas further. But no matter who the client is, I always try to set the tone early on.

When starting a new project, I'll say something like:

"I'd love your feedback to be descriptive and objective, what you liked, what you didn't, and why."

And yes, sometimes there's hand holding involved and that's okay, especially in the early stages of a relationship. Asking questions throughout helps guide the process and keeps everyone aligned.

When I get to the tenth revision and the client still isn't satisfied, I stop and ask myself:

Am I solving the right problem? Or … does the client

not know what they actually want? That's a tough place to be but it happens.

Then there's the dreaded "I just don't like it," with no explanation. That kind of feedback used to crush me. But over time, I realized it's not about me. It's about them. They're struggling to express what's in their head. I help them find the words. I ask questions to find out what they don't like, listen, and adjust gently.

When I deliver a revised design, I've learned to keep my explanations short. One or two lines to summarize the changes at most, especially if I didn't take all the feedback literally. If something felt off or wouldn't work, I'll say that I made a creative adjustment and explain why, in one clear, professional sentence. I try not to over-defend or over-explain. If the work needs too much justification, it probably isn't strong enough yet.

Over time, I've noticed patterns in how leaders give feedback. You start to see the same tendencies in different people. And even now, after years in the business, I'll admit, it can still be tough to receive critiques. But I take a breath and remind myself: this is part of the process and how we get better. Because feedback, when you're open to it, can turn a good design into a great one. And if no one's giving you feedback? That's when you should worry. Ask for it, invite it in. It may sting at first, but in the end, it's the best teacher you'll ever have.

LEARNING TO TRUST YOUR GUT

When I first started in graphic design, I struggled with insecurity, as if I didn't make that clear earlier. I wanted to do well, but I didn't have the experience or the confidence to fully trust my creative instincts. During one of my early weekly meetings with my manager, she asked how I was feeling about the design work I was doing. I told her honestly, I wasn't sure if I was making the right design decisions, I didn't want to fail.

What she said next stuck with me ever since. She said, "You need to trust your gut. You have a talent that not many people possess. You instinctively know what works and what doesn't, you just need to believe that you do."

That was an aha moment! From then on, I made it part of my creative DNA to trust that the solutions

I was coming up with weren't random, they were built on instinct, experience, and passion.

She didn't have to say anything during our meeting. But she did, because she was the kind of leader who saw people, not just employees. Her words gave me permission to believe in myself, and I'll always be grateful to her for that. We have stayed in touch through the years, and I still consider her one of the most inspiring people I've worked with.

WHEN OPPORTUNITY KNOCKS, OPEN THE DOOR

About three years after my first gig as a graphic designer, I received a life-changing opportunity: to work at ESPN in Florida during the time they owned the Bass Anglers Sportsman Society (B.A.S.S.) and ESPN Outdoors. I had applied for jobs there before and never got called in for interviews. The experience mirrored my earlier attempts to get into feature animation, discouraging and defeating. I couldn't help but feel that being Latino and openly gay had something to do with it. My name is also hard to pronounce and once I was told that people would not hire me because my name was almost unpronounceable. Naturally, for me the hiring process became emotionally exhausting and deeply biased.

But then, out of nowhere, the perfect position opened up, it was for a Senior Designer position. I applied with zero expectations. By that point, rejection had become familiar, almost routine. I had reached a point of emotional detachment, so when I got the call for an interview, I didn't let myself get too hopeful. Ironically, that's when it finally worked and I was offered the job.

I'll never forget the interview with the vice president of Marketing. She was refreshingly honest, even cautioning me that the organization wasn't doing well financially and that rocky times might lie ahead. That should have been a red flag, but I saw it as a doorway. I felt like I had outgrown my previous role, and this was a chance to challenge myself in ways I hadn't before.

When I arrived at ESPN, the business was expanding rapidly, but they were facing a major problem: brand inconsistency. Each tournament had its own visual identity, and there was no cohesion linking them back to B.A.S.S. or the parent brand Bassmaster, so everything felt disjointed.

One day, my supervisor brought me into a meeting and showed me a set of concepts created by an external branding firm. They had been tasked with developing a unifying brand architecture for the Bassmaster tournament series. As I flipped through their work, I felt a sinking sense of disappointment. The designs were poorly thought out, disconnected from the culture of the sport, and, frankly, uninspired. I couldn't understand why leadership had outsourced such an important task, especially when we had a talented internal team eager for the opportunity.

I voiced my concerns honestly, and after a few minutes of discussion, I asked if I could take a crack at it myself. My supervisor took the idea to leadership, and soon after, I was given two weeks to develop brand concepts to present directly to the president.

I threw myself into the work by researching car and boat logos, I built mood boards and sketched relentlessly. The biggest challenge was developing a single, unified logo format that could represent five very different tournament brands. I looked at bass fishing boats and was inspired by the silhouette viewed from the front, low, flat, and powerful. That shape became the foundation for the system.

I designed two concepts. One mimicked the silhouette

BEFORE BRAND REFRESH

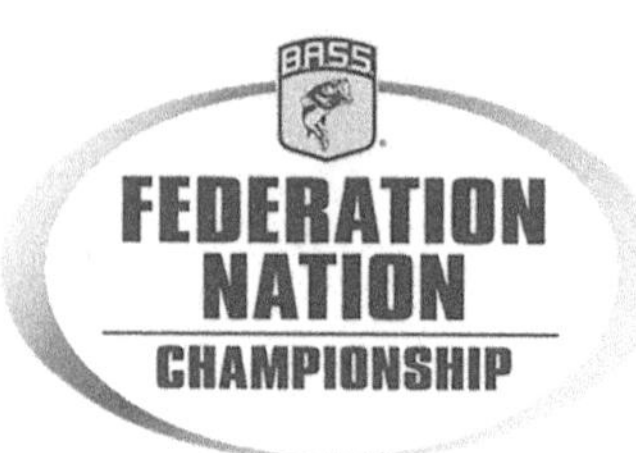

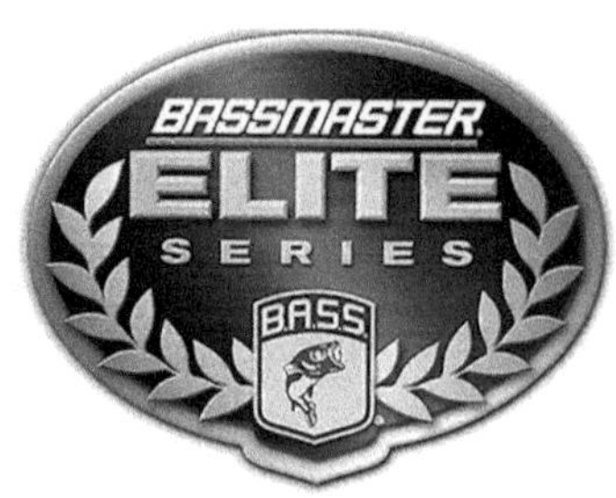

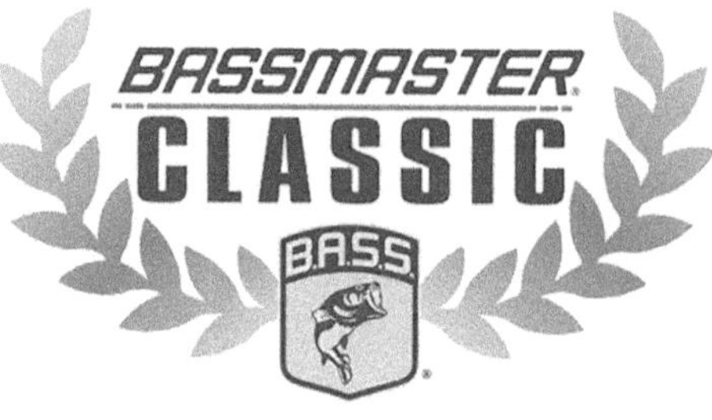

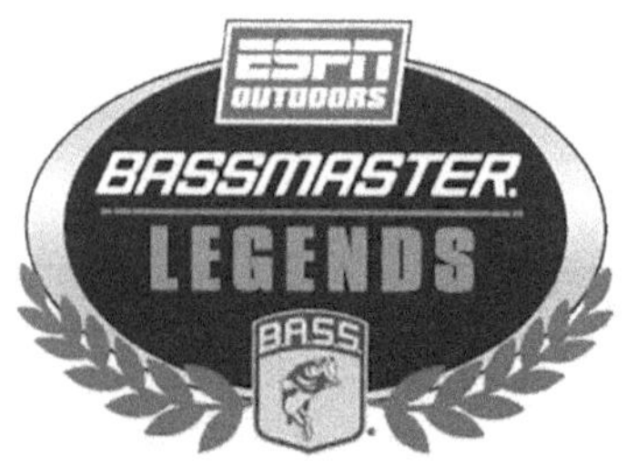

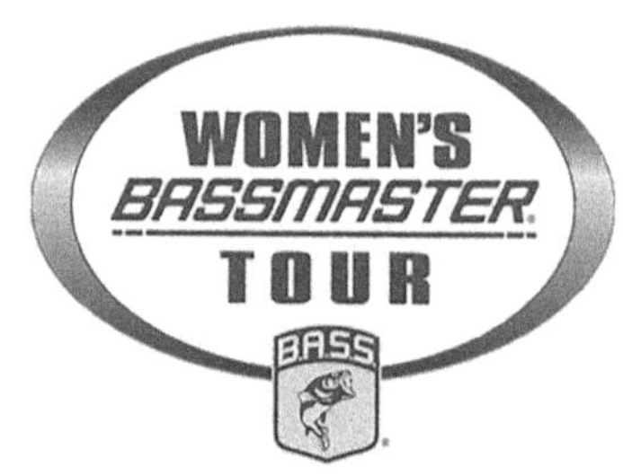

AFTER BRAND REFRESH

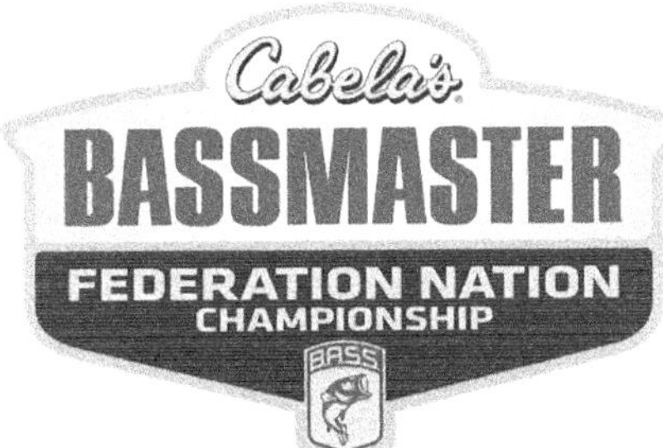
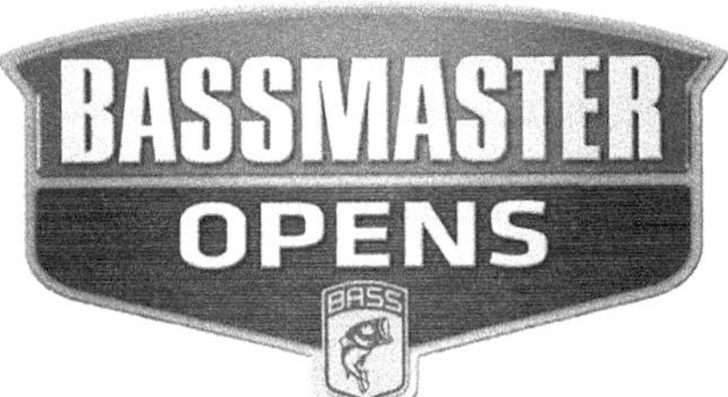
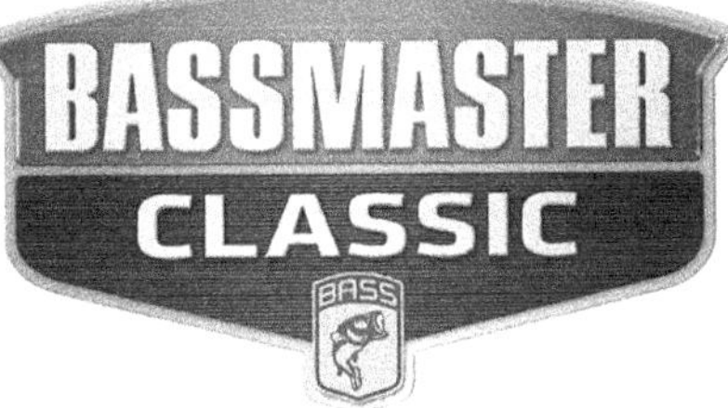
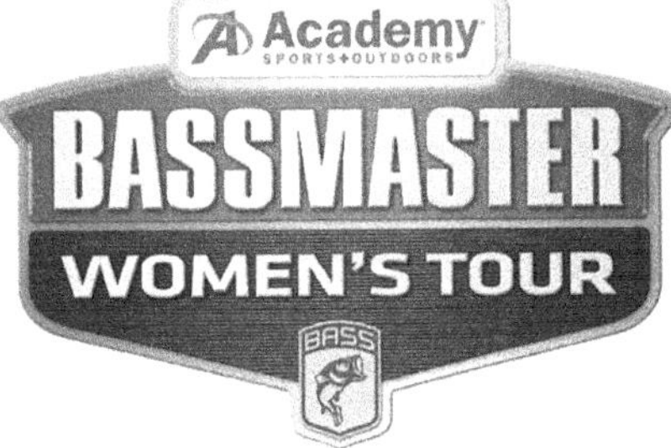
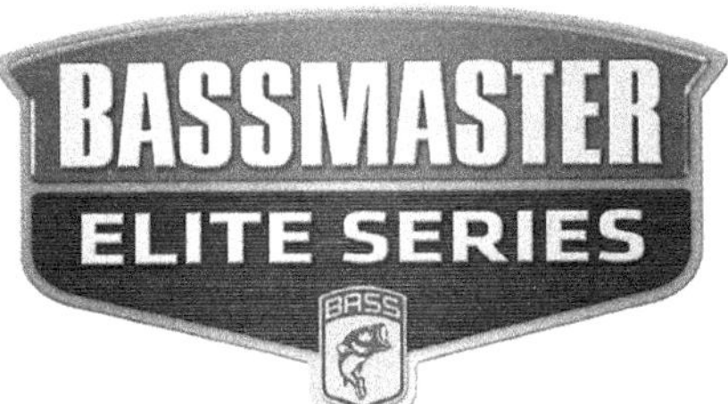

of the existing Elite Series logo, and the other was a completely new shape based on that boat silhouette. It was bold, modern, and clean, with distinct zones to house the tournament name, the Bassmaster brand name, and the B.A.S.S. emblem. I held my breath as I prepared to present it.

To my surprise and delight, the president and ESPN Outdoors leadership enthusiastically chose the boat-shaped concept. They scrapped the outside firm's work entirely and asked me to develop a full brand system based on my design. It was one of the most validating moments of my career. I was even awarded a special bonus for saving the company significant costs and leading such an impactful initiative that changed the direction of the brand forever.

I went on to develop five distinct tournament marks using a color hierarchy inspired by competitive sports: bronze for the Opens, silver for the Elite Series, and gold for the Classic. The Women's Series was given a bold red-pink palette, and the grassroots Federation Nation mark took on a flat gray-blue tone to distinguish it from the others. I used metal textures and 3D elements to modernize the identity, elevating the brand into something dynamic and memorable.

During my time at ESPN, I also had the chance to art direct advertising, including magazine spreads and exclusive Hallmark ornaments. I collaborated with writers, photographers, and fellow designers across the country, an experience that gave me creative confidence and camaraderie I'd never known before.

Then, everything changed. One year later, we were called into a meeting and told that ESPN had sold B.A.S.S. to Don Logan and two other investors. The entire ESPN Outdoors operation would be shut down. We were given the choice to relocate to Alabama to continue with B.A.S.S., or part ways. I had no personal interest in sports or fishing, yet I had grown to love the culture, the challenge, and the incredible team. This was a devastating moment in my career.

Moving to Alabama wasn't realistic for me. I had been under the Disney umbrella for over 15 years at that point and wasn't ready to uproot my life. So, I began searching for other internal Disney opportunities and thankfully shortly thereafter, I found one.

By some twist of fate, I returned to the company's credit union, where I had previously worked during my early days living in California. This time, I returned as the lead creative. It was a full-circle moment. The institution had just completed a merger and needed to develop a new brand identity. I jumped in headfirst, designing the logo, building the style guide, and defining the new visual language. By now, I had grown confident in my design skills, and I leaned into that experience fully.

The department had become more structured and corporate than I remembered. Under the leadership of a new vice president, it was clear I had walked into a new phase of my career. I was trusted with big initiatives right away, including new stationery systems, advertising campaigns, a brand-new membership program, and even the design of a mobile branch. With a bold red and silver palette, I had everything I needed to build something lasting and strong.

What started with a surprise phone call for a job I didn't think I'd get at ESPN became one of the most creatively fulfilling chapters of my career, and the spark that led me into a new era of design leadership.

LEADING WITHOUT THE TITLE

While working at the credit union, and evolved in my design career, I began to wonder what it would be like to become an art director or creative director. I wanted to grow and challenge myself beyond the individual projects I was assigned. I brought this up with several mentors over the years, and they gave me honest feedback: I'd have to let go of some of the hands-on design work in order to focus on vision, leadership, legal concerns, meetings, and a whole lot of paperwork. That didn't sound appealing to me. And frankly, I wasn't sure I'd be good at it but one thing came out of those conversations that surprised me: I realized I was already leading.

As designers, we shape the visual voice of the organizations we work for. We're not handed step-by-step instructions. We use our creativity, instincts, and expertise to build something meaningful, whether it's a brand, a campaign, or a social cause. That is leadership. We don't just execute ideas, we guide the way things are seen and experienced.

I didn't fully understand this until I worked on the Bassmaster brand reboot. That project changed the entire trajectory of the brand, and I did it through initiative and vision, not because someone gave me a title. That's leadership in its purest form.

One of the smartest managers I've worked with, Kathy, once told me: "It's not about titles. Some people with big titles can't keep a staff because they don't know how to lead. It's not about telling people what to do. There are people volunteering across the world with no titles at all, they're leaders because they take something they believe in and do something good with it. You're a leader because you take a scribbled idea on paper and turn it into an amazing campaign."

She also encouraged me to keep doing something I had started naturally: hosting monthly creative inspiration meetings. I'd pick a topic and invite the team to contribute work, ideas, or thoughts tied to that theme.

It became a space where trust grew, ideas flowed, and collaboration flourished. We built a kind of creative idea bank, and people began sharing more freely in their own projects because of the openness we created there. And guess what happened, we borrowed many of the ideas born from those conversations and brainstorms for some amazing campaign work. That's leadership too.

THE OTHER SIDE OF LEADERSHIP

As I learned more about creative leadership, I met with several art directors and creative directors. I asked how they managed giving up the design work they loved. One told me he enjoyed the variety, his day was never the same. He went from meetings to client calls to creative reviews and loved the rhythm. Another, who ran his own design studio, said that even though designing was his passion, leading meant letting go so others could shine.

That's when I realized: leading teams isn't for everyone, and that's okay.

I came to learn that while I could lead, I didn't necessarily want the job title. But that didn't mean I couldn't support others.

In one of my roles, I got the chance to work with

freelancers and interns. I assigned projects, gave feedback, and helped guide their development. It was a shift, being the one giving direction instead of receiving it. I'll be honest: it wasn't easy. I often wanted to just do the work myself. I knew how I'd handle it, I knew it would be faster, but that wasn't the assignment. My role was to support them and help them grow.

It took time, practice, and patience. I had to unlearn habits of independence and embrace the challenge of mentorship. I stopped telling and started asking. I shared knowledge and I offered guidance instead of directives. Eventually, it got easier and more rewarding.

I also learned that leadership is about more than the work, it's about understanding people. Everyone is their own island, with their own goals, dreams, and insecurities. Part of being a strong leader is recognizing who's ready for what and helping match projects to passions.

The more I let go, the more I understood what real creative leadership looked like.

And in doing so, I saw something beautiful: the same trust that once built me as a designer, I was now passing on to others.

HOW TO SPOT A TOXIC LEADER (AND WHAT ONE TAUGHT ME)

There was a time in my career when I was genuinely enjoying my job. I had a supportive leader, a healthy team dynamic, and a strong sense of creative purpose. But that all changed when my then-leader John decided to bring in someone new, an old colleague of his from a former job, whom I'll call Mark.

From the very first call I had with him, Mark set off alarm bells. He talked a lot about himself. He boasted about his accolades and referred to himself as an "award-winning designer," though he was more interested in control than creativity. He dismissed all the work our team had done before he arrived, often in condescending and downright offensive ways. It wasn't long before we realized that he didn't actually understand the realities of our design processes or budget. He just wanted to leave his mark, pun intended.

Mark wasn't interested in leading; he just wanted to dominate. His style was crude, aggressive, and deeply insecure. He belittled ideas, questioned my professionalism, criticized my demeanor, and even mocked my personal values. His behavior created a toxic atmosphere that slowly drove a wedge through the team. He didn't want collaboration, he wanted obedience.

As the years went by, things didn't get any better, they actually turned for the worst. One time, Mark invited his team to a luncheon at a local restaurant. He was based in California and rarely visited our Orlando office. I arrived at the restaurant early and waited at the entrance. When Mark showed up, he was glued to his phone, completely disengaged from his surroundings. He saw me, but yet he still walked right past me, no eye contact, no hello, not even a nod of acknowledgment. At first, I assumed he might be dealing with something urgent. But minutes later, I discovered he wasn't answering emails or handling work, he was playing a silly mobile game. That game was more deserving of his attention than greeting one of his own team members, someone who had taken the time to be there early and ready to connect.

Unfortunately, this wasn't an isolated incident. It simply reinforced a pattern I had already observed and experienced: he had no real interest in building relationships, no desire to lead with presence or respect. I was one of the most senior creatives on his team, and yet I felt invisible. Sometimes, toxic leadership doesn't scream. It shrugs, scrolls, and ignores. That, too, leaves damage in its wake.

Despite this, I stayed, not because I was comfortable, but because I believed in the mission of the organization, and I had worked too hard and for too many years to let someone like him push me out. So, I held on, and so did the stress.

Over time, more than 22 people left the department. HR complaints piled up. He was written up, repeatedly. His peers didn't respect him; in fact, many mocked him behind closed doors. Eventually, after nine long years, he was terminated but by then, only three of us remained, and I was the only one left from the original team.

What kept me going through all of that wasn't just stubbornness, it was the support I received from other leaders across the company who knew what I was going through. And it was a simple belief: nothing lasts forever. I told myself that every day.

I learned more about leadership in those years than I ever imagined. Because sometimes the worst leaders show you, with painful clarity, what leadership should never be. Mark wasn't just a bad boss, he was a cautionary tale. And his boss, John, who allowed it all to happen? Just as complicit even though he was aware of the problem.

You can usually spot a toxic leader pretty quickly, if you're paying attention. It starts with how they treat you the moment you walk in the door. Are they respectful? Do they listen? Are their questions thoughtful or dismissive? Do they seem interested in your story, or are they just scanning your résumé for flaws? And if you get the chance, observe how they treat their own staff. Body language and tone can say a lot, and even if people don't speak openly, their eyes often will.

Toxic leaders are everywhere. They're easy to spot, mainly because no one likes working for them. And yes,

I say "for them", not "with them", because they rarely treat others as peers. They hoard power, expect blind obedience, and often use intimidation to maintain control. These people tend to rise through titles, not talent. They confuse fear with respect.

I learned all this the hard way.

But wait, there's more. One day, Mark asked me and a colleague from the team to review and completely rewrite a newsletter that had come from an external organization. He also wanted us to redesign the layout and give it a fresh, more polished look. At the time, we had no idea why he was making this request, it was out of the blue and unlike anything we'd been asked to do before. Still, we dropped everything, made it a priority, and poured our energy into getting it right. At some point, my colleague asked what the piece was going to be used for. Mark casually replied that he planned to share it with the organization as a favor, to give them some ideas on how they could improve their newsletter.

We completed the project and handed off the final document. He didn't thank us, didn't acknowledge the effort we had put in. Later, we found out the real reason for the assignment, he had presented the rewritten and redesigned newsletter as his own work to the organization, using it to position himself as a thought leader and ultimately securing an advisory role with them. We weren't just left out of the credit, we were used.

WHAT REAL LEADERSHIP LOOKS LIKE

For contrast, let me tell you about a recent leader I was fortunate to work with. I hadn't been in this new area of the company for very long, but I had already contributed significantly to work that was helping grow the brand. When it came time to share our progress at a company-wide town hall, something unexpected happened: instead of my vice president taking the spotlight or delivering the presentation herself, as many leaders might, she asked me to present the work. She said it was important that I be the one to share it, because I had been directly involved in making it happen.

She didn't have to do that. She could have presented the work, spoken broadly about the team, and still looked like a strong leader. But she believed in elevating the people around her. She believed in giving credit where it was due. That's what real leadership looks like.

Real leaders don't hoard applause, they share it. They don't silence or overshadow their teams, they amplify them. They protect you when it matters, challenge you when it counts, and most of all, they lead with empathy.

The difference between a good leader and a toxic one can shape not just your career, but your sense of self. I know, because I've lived both.

So, if you ever find yourself in a room with someone who thinks leadership is about yelling, belittling, or manipulating, do yourself a favor: walk out of that room because you deserve better, we all do.

WHERE DO CREATIVE IDEAS COME FROM?

I have been asked this question, and I have also considered it many times. I wish I had a perfect answer to this question. But the truth is, I don't really know.

What I do know is that creativity is connected to everything you're exposed to in life, your experiences, your memories, and your subconscious mind. When I was a young designer, new to the field, generating ideas was much harder than it is now. With time and experience, ideas don't just appear faster, they feel more complete, more intuitive.

I believe anyone pursuing a creative life should seek out the world. Immerse yourself in it. Explore art, culture, music, and history. Visit galleries, museums, film screenings, plays, operas, ballets. Read. Watch. Listen. Let it all in. You never know what might move you or awaken something deep inside.

For me, it started with music. My parents loved classical music, and I grew up listening to it constantly. Instead of watching television, my mom would play instrumental records. That early exposure gave me the gift of imagination, I remember composing full symphonic movements in my head as a child. Even today, I work to the sounds of contemporary composers like Jóhann Jóhannsson, James Newton Howard, or Mason Bates. That music becomes a kind of fuel for my creativity.

Art has also left a deep imprint in me. When I studied art history in university, I was introduced to Van Gogh's work. I understood the concept of visual rhythm, but I didn't feel it until I stood in front of his painting *The Mulberry Tree* at the Norton Simon Museum in Pasadena. It hit me like lightning. The leaves seemed to sway in the breeze. The thick, swirling paint looked fresh, alive. I started to shake, and I wept quietly so no one would notice. I had never been moved like that by a painting. And to this day, when I'm in Pasadena, I visit

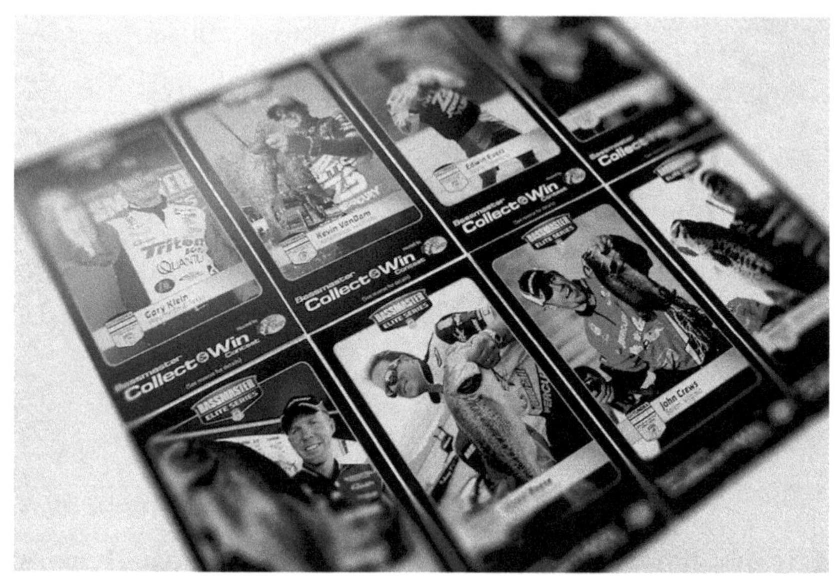

Bassmaster Elite Series Angler Collectible Card Set, 2010 ©B.A.S.S.

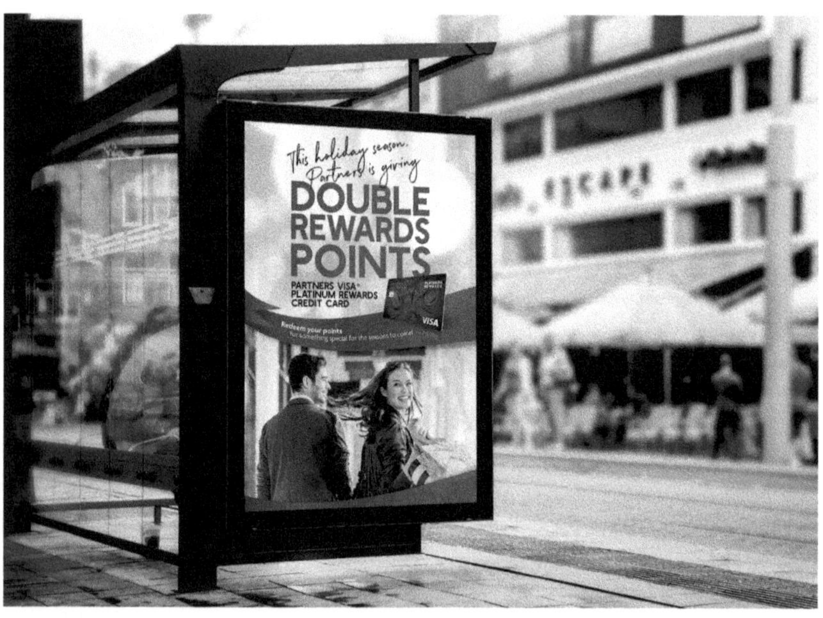

Partners Federal Credit Union Double Rewards Credit Card Offer, 2018
©Disney

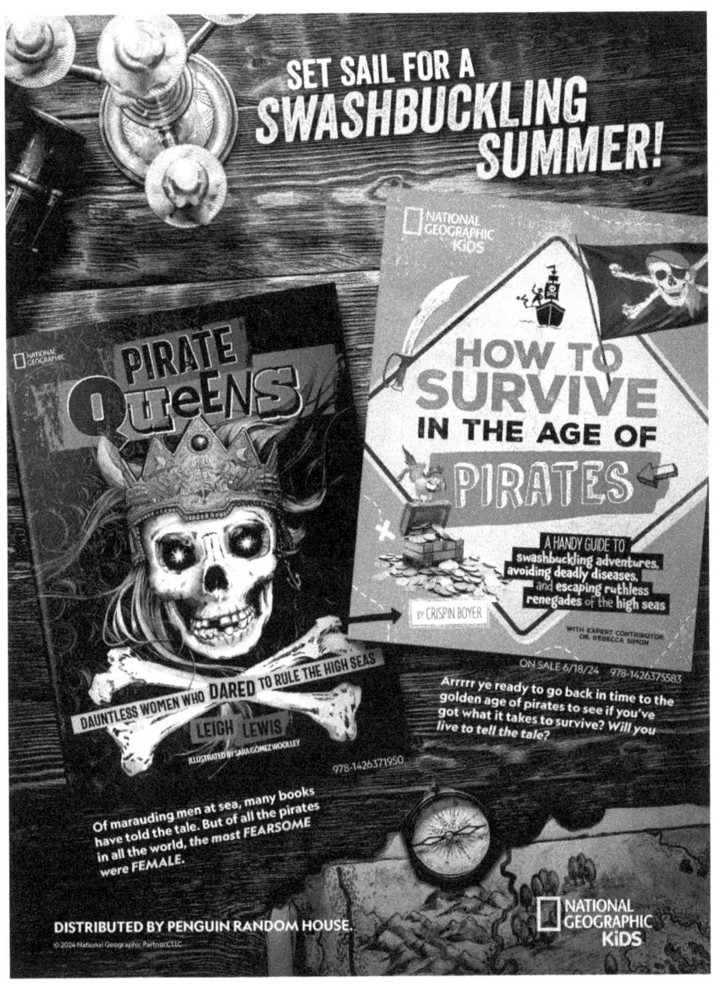

National Geographic Kids Pirate Books Print Advertising, 2024
©National Geographic Kids

The Mulberry Tree, just to feel it again.

More recently, that same kind of magic happened while watching Puccini's Madama Butterfly on PBS. I grew up listening to opera in the background, so I recognized the music right away. I began to watch the performance and became completely immersed in the story, costumes, music, amazing talent, and the simplicity and creativity of the sets. During the final act, as Cio-Cio-San took her life, I found myself sobbing. I wasn't being dramatic, it was instinctive, like breathing. The performance pierced me, and I rarely cry at anything on screen.

That's the power of art. That's the kind of impact I hope to make through my own work, whether it's a design, a painting, a piece of writing, or a social media post. I know it's hard to generate that level of emotion through a marketing ad, but I believe it's possible to move people in small, meaningful ways. Because if a painting or an aria can reach into your soul, why not your work?

When I mentor others, I always ask them to show me a piece of art they love. It can be anything, a sculpture, a photo, or a poster. I ask why they love it and what it makes them feel. Their answers are always surprising, and deeply personal. For some it's a two-thousand-year-old

Egyptian gold snake bracelet. For others, it's a painting of a boat at sea by an anonymous artist. What inspires us is shaped by everything we've ever been exposed to, especially the things that made us feel something.

To me, creativity is built from that collection of personal moments. A kind of mental library. I think of it as my bag of tricks, a space filled with stories, colors, sounds, techniques, memories, textures, and instincts that I draw from every time I sit down to make something.

And then there's the subconscious.

When I get a new design brief, I rarely dive in right away. I read it carefully, take it in, and then I walk away. I let it breathe. I sleep on it. And almost always, by the next morning, the solution has already taken shape. I wake up, and the idea is just there, fully formed, like a gift waiting to be unwrapped. Sometimes I still need to ask a few more questions to fill in the gaps, but the foundation is already built quietly in the background of my mind. The more experience you have, the easier it becomes to shape visual solutions before you even sit down at your desk. I often say, "The work is done in my head, I just need to let it out."

I don't know exactly how to explain that part. Maybe

it's just how our brains process information. Or maybe it's something more. I call it the subconscious because that's the word that makes the most sense. But maybe … it's magic.

YOU ARE NOT A FRAUD, YOU'RE JUST GROWING

> *"I have written eleven books, but each time I think, 'Uh oh, they're going to find out now."*
> — Maya Angelou

"When are they going to find out I'm a fake?" That thought hit me the day I got my first design job. When I got hired for my first graphic design job, I had a terrifying thought: Impostor syndrome. It hit me hard. I told myself: "They made a mistake. I'm not actually qualified. I probably oversold myself in the interview." I even considered calling to tell them I wasn't the right fit before day one. But I didn't.

I showed up on my first day, nervous, grateful, and filled with self-doubt. The first project I worked on had me convinced I'd get fired immediately. But I didn't so I kept going. Slowly, with each task, I started to realize I could do this. The fear quieted down. The skills I had weren't imaginary, they were real.

I still remember thinking: "This is actually easy. I can do this with my eyes closed." And just like that, my confidence began to take root. But here's the honest truth: I still feel impostor syndrome sometimes. Even after years in the field. Even after big wins. Even after being praised and promoted. That's the thing no one tells you: impostor syndrome doesn't always go away; it just changes shape.

I've learned that insecurity is a natural part of being human. In fact, if someone tells you they're 100% confident all the time, they're probably faking it. Doubt shows you care, and it shows you're invested in doing meaningful work. What matters is what you do with that doubt. I let mine fuel me to keep growing, keep learning, and keep showing up.

If you're feeling like a fraud, take a breath. You're not faking it, you're just learning to believe in yourself.

FINDING WHERE YOU BELONG

Everyone wants to feel part of something. Well, almost everyone. That sense of belonging, not just showing up but being seen and valued, is quietly powerful.

I once worked with a colleague who was incredibly talented and experienced. I often brainstormed with him because he had such a deep understanding of the business. But for him, the job wasn't a passion, it was just work. He designed to support his family. He didn't care about team dynamics or being part of something larger. He was the classic lone wolf: do great work, then disappear to go fishing at lunch. And that was enough for him and there is nothing wrong with that.

For me, it was different. I've always felt a deeper drive. I need to solve creative problems. When I'm not designing, my brain aches. I genuinely love what I do. And while I've never needed to be the center of attention, I've always longed to belong. In school, I didn't connect with typical social groups. I watched my classmates play soccer and wondered why I wasn't drawn to the same things. Later in college, I felt like an outsider until I got the part in *Hello, Dolly!* That moment of inclusion, the simple act of being cast, lit something inside me. I was finally part of something, and it felt amazing, I belonged.

I've carried that longing into adulthood. When I worked in animation, I often felt like I was standing outside the windows looking in, watching the cool guys doing all the fun work, never fully invited in. Even though I was doing related animation work, I didn't feel like I belonged. That "outsider looking in" mindset became a quiet, painful complex.

But in hindsight, that outsider feeling may have been a gift. Because it pushed me toward something better.

When I started studying graphic design in the online program, I threw myself into it. After work, I studied obsessively. I practiced, experimented, and built my skills piece by piece. Later, while working in my first graphic design job, I was able to complete my fine arts degree through the company's education reimbursement program. It was a slow build, but I could feel the shift, I was improving, and I knew it.

Then came my first Adobe MAX conference. I was surrounded by people like me, people who spoke the same visual language, who understood the creative process, who were excited to learn, build, and evolve. For the first time, I didn't feel like an outsider. I belonged to something bigger than myself.

I found my people. And with that came a deeper truth: not only could I belong, I could lead, influence, and help others find their place, too.

Sometimes you find your place not by fitting in, but by creating the space where you finally feel seen.

REDEFINING SUCCESS

Success is personal, it doesn't always look like a promotion, a trophy, or a title. Sometimes, it shows up as peace, as fulfillment, as finally being seen and valued for who you are and what you bring.

When I left ESPN, I already felt I had achieved a version of success. I was confident in my skills, fairly paid, and creatively engaged. Even after many years of designing similar campaigns, each project still felt fresh and that mattered to me. That was my personal barometer of success: to still be growing, still challenged, and still passionate about the work.

Later in my career, I applied for a publishing role within the company, a position that almost never opened up in my region. I had always admired that part of the organization, but never thought it was within reach.

Quietly and hopefully, I submitted my application, fine-tuned my designer-style résumé, and waited. To my surprise, I got an interview.

Alex, the hiring manager, had already seen my portfolio and was familiar with my work. In fact, he specifically remembered a campaign I had created for Hispanic Heritage Month, one I had volunteered for and poured my heart into. That project had stayed with him. He even read the case study I wrote about it on my website delaespriella.com.

The moment I realized he had really seen my work, and saw me, something shifted. We had a fantastic conversation for over an hour. We were both artists, and our creative values aligned. It wasn't just another interview, it felt like a genuine connection. After a few more rounds, and waiting … I was offered the job.

I'll never forget how I felt when I got that call. It wasn't just relief, it was validation. Once again, I didn't get there because I "knew someone". I got there because of my talent, my persistence, and the work I had put in over decades. I was hired not in spite of my experience, but because of it.

In my new role, I was trusted, respected, and

challenged creatively. Again, I felt like I belonged, not just as a designer, but as a person.

Later that year, during my performance review, Alex, himself a seasoned creative, told me something that will stay with me forever. He said that my work had elevated the team's creative output in ways they hadn't seen before. That I had helped shape the brand in a lasting, meaningful way and that others looked up to me and my work for inspiration.

I don't walk around thinking "I'm successful" every day. But in that moment, I did. And that was enough.

MENTORING

I had my first real exposure to mentoring later in my career when I applied to be a mentee through an employee resource group at work. I had never been formally mentored before and thought it could be a great opportunity to learn more about myself and grow. I had nothing to lose but the time I invested, and it turned out to be one of the most eye-opening professional experiences I've ever had.

The program matched me with a leader in the same design and creativity field. At the kickoff event, we were walked through the program and introduced to our mentors and mentees. I was paired with Bryan, and we clicked immediately. He was the creative editor in chief of an internal company magazine and the right person to guide me during the program. Over the next few months, we met at his office or mine and had deeply moving conversations around growth, leadership, and dealing with difficult dynamics at work.

Bryan helped me manage personal work-related struggles. He didn't sugarcoat anything, but he listened, asked the right questions, and shared thoughtful, challenging feedback that pushed me to grow.

One of the biggest lessons I took away was this: you can't control other people, but you can control how you carry yourself. I learned to let go a bit, to stop holding on so tightly to stress, and to trust that professionalism and emotional steadiness would carry me through.

Bryan also reminded me that I wasn't the only voice in the room. As designers, we work with many people, our ability to listen, collaborate, and include others is just as important as our creative vision.

The mentorship experience not only helped me grow professionally, but it also resulted in a meaningful friendship I truly cherish. If you ever have the opportunity to participate in a mentoring program, take it. The work you do on yourself now can shape your future in ways you can't yet imagine.

Years later, I felt it was time to give back. As the world began to reemerge from the pandemic, I applied to be a mentor through the American Institute of Graphic Arts

(AIGA) New York chapter, and was accepted. That on its own was a thrill.

I was paired with a talented young designer from Brooklyn named Jan. The program was straightforward, but the connection we formed was anything but ordinary. Jan was looking to grow as a designer, expand her creativity and enhance her creative app skills, and I saw this as a perfect opportunity to help her cultivate her voice while continuing to evolve my own understanding of mentorship.

From the beginning, I asked Jan many questions, not just about her work, but about what inspired her, why she was drawn to certain visuals, and how she saw herself growing. You can learn a lot about a designer by what they find inspiring.

She had a great eye, a strong grasp of design foundations, and a curiosity that reminded me of myself at that stage. She shared her recent work, and we discussed the challenges she was facing, especially when navigating complex software like Adobe Photoshop. I could tell the technical side overwhelmed her.

To help her, I shared some of my recent personal projects and broke them down step-by-step. I explained my creative process like a puzzle, each decision leading to the next. This made the path more approachable and the learning more empowering.

Though the official program lasted only six months, we've continued to meet quarterly. Our relationship has grown into an ongoing dialogue of support, insight, and shared growth. Her design work has improved significantly, and more importantly, I can tell how much she values our time together.

I have mentored for two AIGA mentorship programs and many more through my employment history. Yet another layer of design that has been fulfilling in my life.

WHAT'S NEXT

I often ask myself what comes after the 9-to-5. The answer is clear: I will continue to create.

As I approach retirement, I've been exploring new opportunities that let me stay rooted in art and design. Writing, challenging, rewarding, and deeply creative, will absolutely remain part of my journey. I've also begun experimenting with pattern design, especially in fashion accessories like silk scarves and pocket squares. Fashion continues to spark my imagination, so I'm giving that "what if" a real try. Every time I start sketching ideas, I feel a familiar thrill, the same one that's carried me through this career.

One passion I haven't written much about in this book is painting. As explained earlier, I discovered it in the early 2000s, and it felt like opening a window after years indoors. Working in oils, especially, gave me a new sense of freedom. In the next chapter of my life, I plan to take painting more seriously, perhaps even build a new body of work around it.

But above all, I want to keep learning and traveling. The world has so much more to teach me, through different cultures, new perspectives, and unexpected ways of making art. I can't wait to see what I'll discover next. And I know, in my heart, that the creative path I've walked for decades is far from finished.

And yes, I'll continue to mentor, to uplift others, and to give back to the creative community that gave so much to me. The joy of paying it forward will always be part of the work.

CASE STUDY: THE HISPANIC HERITAGE MONTH CELEBRATION

How do you define the rich, diverse culture of Hispanics across the globe in a single, inclusive visual representation?

That was the challenge placed before me when, just a few months earlier, I was honored as a Disney Latino artist with a once-in-a-lifetime opportunity: to lead the creative direction for The Walt Disney Company's 2021 enterprise-wide celebration of the Hispanic Latinx Heritage Month.

When I joined the initial conversations about the campaign, a few design ideas had already been proposed, flags from different countries, decorative tiles inspired by regional motifs, and a muted color palette that, while tasteful, didn't quite reflect the vibrancy of our culture. These concepts had merit, but they felt too safe, too expected. They didn't capture the heart of who we are. We are more than patterns and symbols, we are bold, expressive, and full of color. We are proud. We are loud. And we deserve to be seen that way.

It was during a typical weekend at home in mid-July, doing chores, letting my mind wander, that the ideas began to crystallize. I thought about my childhood in Panama, retracing memories in my mind to see where inspiration might emerge. I reached out to several Latino friends and colleagues, asking them to share stories of their upbringing. The conversations uncovered a beautiful truth: no matter where we grew up, we all shared a deep connection to our land, its scents, sounds, and vibrant natural beauty.

What stood out most from my own memories were the moments out in nature, going to the beach with my family, or walking near the Río Piedra in Colón, close to where I was born. I remembered the unmistakable calls of the "guacamayas" (macaws) and many other birds echoing through the air as if announcing their presence, "Here we are, look at me." Their dazzling feathers, flashing brilliant gradients of color in the sunlight, felt like a perfect metaphor for our community: bold, varied, unforgettable. And as it turned out, many of my friends had similar memories of native birds, plants, and landscapes that left a lasting impression.

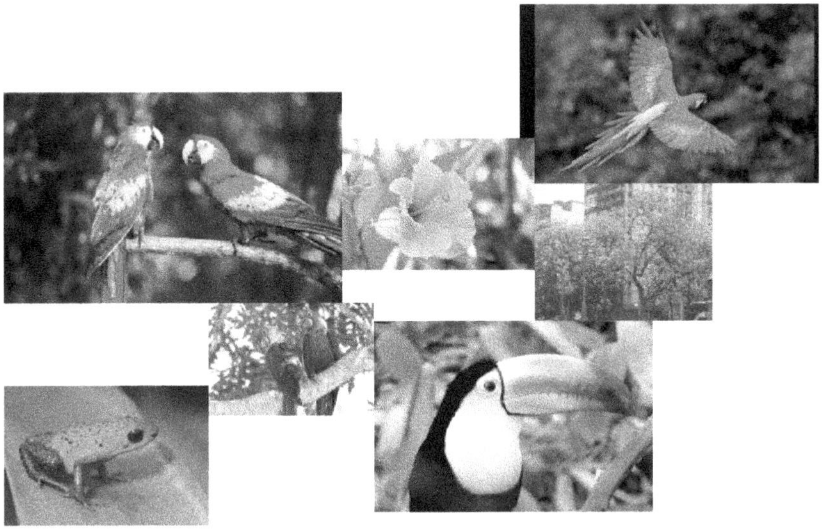

Flora and fauna found all across Latin America.

COLOR STORY

Color can express individuality, it can reflect the mood of a person or the essence of a story. In Disney storytelling, color plays an incredibly important role. Every scene in a film is carefully crafted with a color script that helps communicate the emotional state of the characters, often mirrored in the environment, from the background to the costumes to the lighting that fills the space. As I considered how we use color in visual storytelling, I began to see it not just as decoration, but as an emotional cue, a way to emphasize ideas, convey attitudes, and elevate the underlying themes that give a narrative its heart.

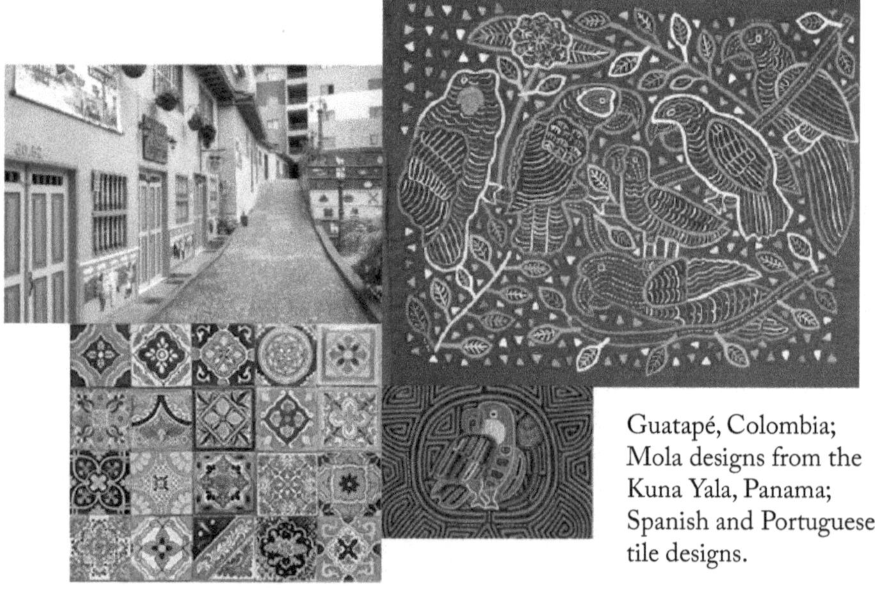

Guatapé, Colombia; Mola designs from the Kuna Yala, Panama; Spanish and Portuguese tile designs.

Then I began to make color connections to my culture. In Latin America, we paint our homes in bright, joyful colors; we dress the same way, with bold patterns and vibrant fabrics, and we speak with more volume and energy than most, perhaps to match the intensity of the tropical sun. Across our many countries and traditions, color is revered, not only as something visual, but as something deeply emotional and symbolic. You see it in the folklore and the elaborate dresses like the Polleras of Panama, in the vividly painted homes of Guatapé, Colombia, in the intricate azulejos of Spain and Portugal, and in how Mexican culture celebrates death not with darkness, but with vibrancy, honoring life with color and spirit. Our cultures celebrate color every day, in what we wear, in how we decorate our spaces, and in the warmth and generosity we extend to one another through every tone of our lives.

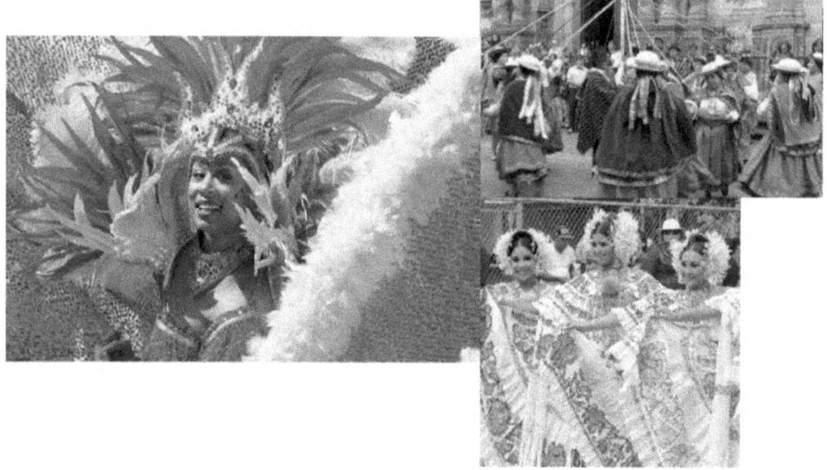

Use of color dominates the beautiful folklore of the Hispanic Latinx culture as seen in these examples.

It became clear that color would be the foundation for representing our rich heritage. And what better way to express that than by paying homage to the macaws, the brilliant gradient of colors they carry across their feathers is a natural symbol of who we are. But there's more to macaws than just their beauty. Like us, most macaws mate for life. They share their food with their partners, they groom and care for each other, and they are known for being both intelligent and deeply social creatures. Their yellow facial feathers, unique to each bird, are as distinct as our fingerprints, a quiet reminder of our individuality within a shared culture.

There's something almost magical that happens when you examine a macaw's feathers closely. No single feather holds just one color. Instead, each one carries layers that blend together in harmony, like a chorus of united voices *(Voces Unidas)* forming something more powerful and beautiful than any single note could on its own. With that inspiration, I created the Disney enterprise's Hispanic Latinx Heritage Month design. It is a story told from my heart to every person across the company and beyond. This isn't just a celebration of our culture, it's a reflection of our sacrifices, our struggles, our love for family and community, and most of all, our shared celebration of life.

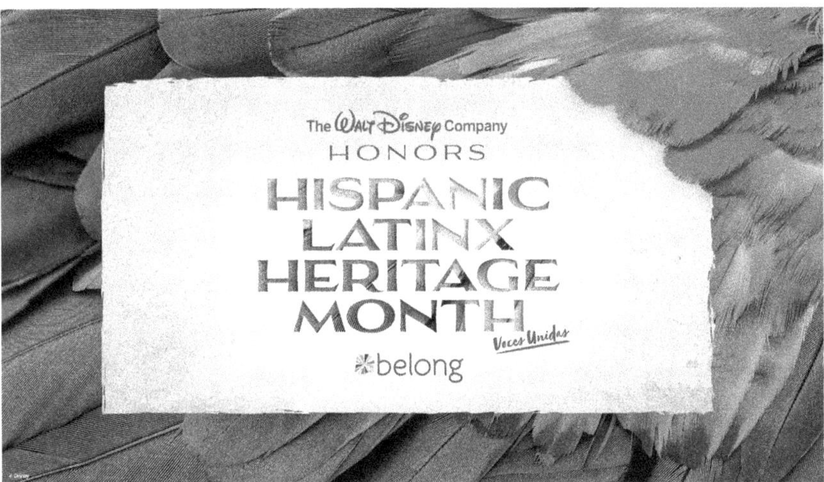

Final design for the Hispanic Latinx Heritage Month.

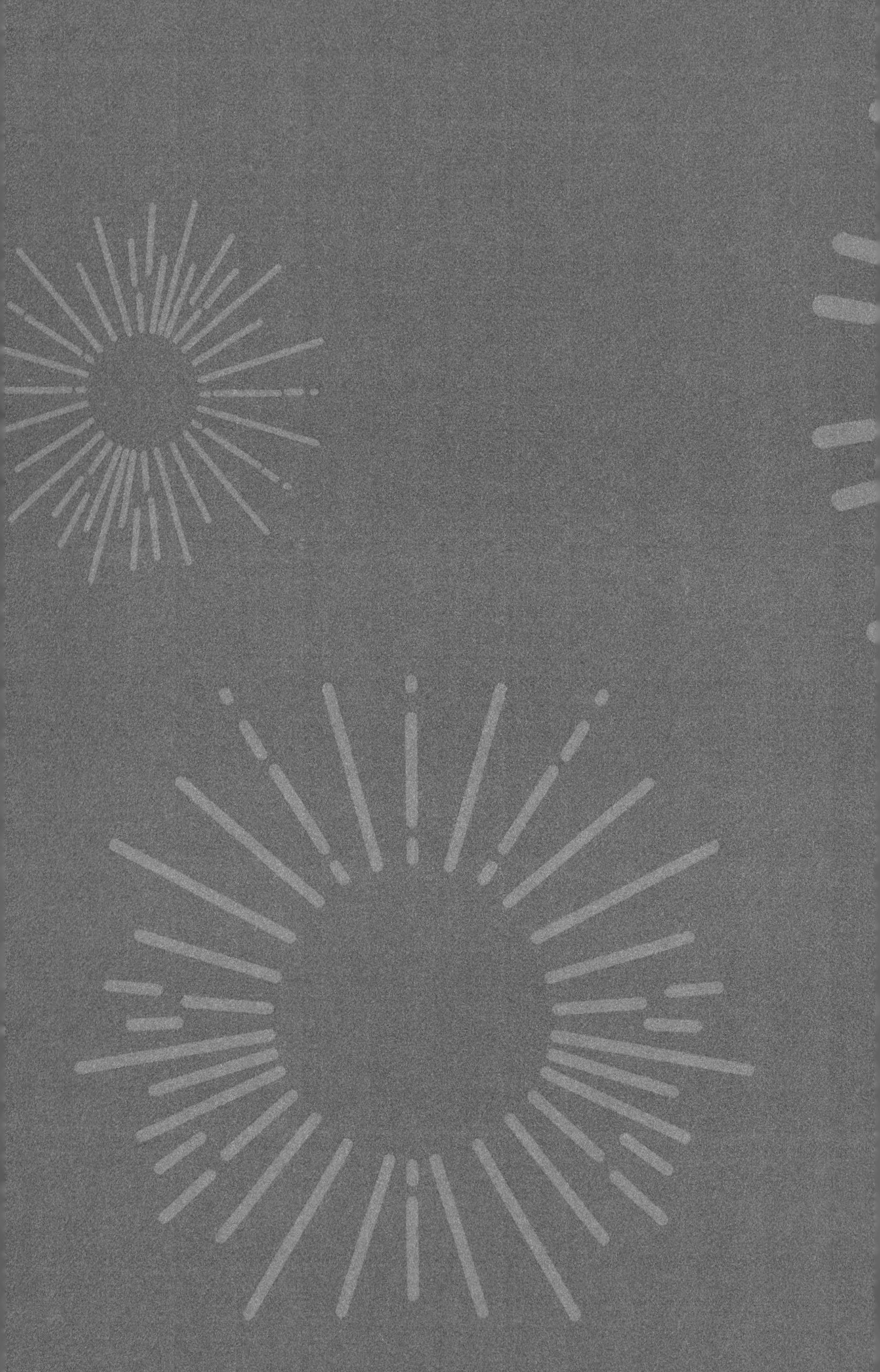

THE CREATIVE SPARK PRINCIPLES

PART TWO

THE CREATIVE SPARK PRINCIPLES

My guiding principles for building a meaningful, resilient, and inspired design career.

Before reaching my 30-year career milestone, I decided to write a post reflecting on the journey to celebrate the special occasion, not just on my blog, but also on my LinkedIn profile. At first, I considered the usual "look back" approach, sharing highs or telling favorite stories, but I wanted to do something different where I could share knowledge. I started thinking about the lessons I've learned, the values I've held onto, and the advice I often find myself giving to others. That's when the idea of creating a set of design principles came to life. What began as a simple list with brief descriptions for that article slowly evolved. The principles you see here today are a deeper, more personal version of that original list, expanded through storytelling, reflection, and experience.

Think of these design principles as a creative survival kit, part compass, part spell book. They're not rules, and they're not sacred. They're reflections I wrote down after navigating tight deadlines, tough feedback, impossible asks, and career pivots. Some are practical, others more philosophical, but all of them are earned.

I share them with the hope that they light a spark for you, especially when you're deep in the work and wondering if you're still on the right path. They're here to remind you that your creativity is a force, that your growth matters, and that sometimes, the smallest principle can cast the biggest magic.

I've separated them into four themes:
- ***Creative Mindset and Personal Growth,***
- ***Design in Practice,***
- ***Relationships and Collaboration, and***
- ***Professionalism and the Workplace.***

FALL FORWARD, FAIL SMARTER

Don't feel bad when you make a mistake. You can't grow without them. Mistakes are how we evolve, as artists, professionals, and people. The key is to make them, learn from them, and avoid making the same ones twice. Every misstep is a moment to become sharper at what you do and clearer about who you are.

I've made plenty of mistakes in my career, and I'm not ashamed to admit it. Early on, I struggled with grammar and copy writing in my design work. I was so focused on the visual aspects of my designs that I'd overlook typos or poorly written messaging. I'd forget to run spell check or double-check the words because I was consumed by color, layout, and balance. But once I faced that weakness head-on, it became a strength. Over time, I improved my eye for messaging and even started contributing stronger copy ideas to enhance the work.

I still make mistakes, especially when I'm moving

too fast or buried in multiple deadlines. And yes, I get frustrated with myself. But I've learned that the real solution is to slow down, even just a little. You can only give your best to one design at a time. Stay present with the project in front of you. Give it your full attention. You'll not only reduce edits, you'll produce work you can be proud of.

Every designer fumbles. But the best ones turn those stumbles into stepping-stones. So don't fear failure. Fall forward and fail smarter next time.

DON'T HOLD BACK

Don't hold yourself back from trying something new just because of what others might think. How would you know if you're good at something, or if you love it, without ever experiencing it?

I never would have discovered how much theater could help me come out of my shell if I hadn't pushed myself to simply show up. That one decision opened a door I didn't even know I needed.

Holding back out of fear of judgment, whether from friends, colleagues, parents, or even complete strangers, is ultimately unfair to yourself. It keeps you from discovering parts of who you are and what you're capable of becoming.

KEEP A DIARY

Back in my youth, I filled the pages of a composition notebook with the memories of my days. My diary wasn't just words, it was a creative playground. I would sketch, design, and most curiously, reimagine movie titles I saw advertised, creating new typographic designs for each one. Looking back, I realize I was desperately seeking outlets for creativity in a world that wasn't offering much inspiration, neither at school nor at home. That diary was a lifeline for me, a healthy and quite a very personal space for expression.

Diaries are an essential part of growing up. Mine was a blend of thoughts and drawings, a private world where I could explore freely. Sadly, in a moment of rage fueled by personal struggles, I destroyed them all. I was quietly suffering after the death of my brother. His absence carved a deep void in my life. We had formed a strong bond, and I must have searched for something, or someone, to fill that space, only to learn that nothing could ever replace his presence. And yet, I kept writing, kept drawing, kept creating. It was how I stayed connected to myself.

Keeping a diary is one of the healthiest habits you can develop. It doesn't have to be just words, it can be sketches, photos, or any collection of memories. Whether in a notebook or a folder on your phone, documenting your inner world helps you revisit who you were and better understand who you're becoming.

STRETCH YOUR PERSPECTIVE

Whether it's another country or just the next town over, stepping outside your everyday surroundings can deepen your understanding of the world and yourself. For me, my first trip to Chicago and later to Miami showed that we weren't just part of Panama, we were part of a much bigger world.

Exposure to other cultures, ideas, and ways of life broadens your creativity and strengthens your empathy.

TAKE THE LEAP BEFORE YOU ARE READY

I've told you the story about how my grandmother once told me to take risks, even when they felt scary. But she didn't mean reckless risks. She meant the kind that are guided by intention, planning, and heart. She didn't want me to reach her age one day and wonder why I never followed my dreams. Her words stayed with me.

Years later, I took one of the biggest calculated risks of my life. I moved from Miami to Orlando without a job lined up, but only a dream to become an artist and the belief that I could make it work. I had saved enough money to live for a few months, researched a place I could afford, and planned every detail down to what I could live without. Once I arrived, I wasted no time. I networked, applied, and put myself out there. A few months later, I landed a job. That leap changed the course of my life.

Later in my career, I took another leap, this time into a role at a company whose future was uncertain. During my time there, I led initiatives that reshaped the brand, created long-lasting impact, and laid the groundwork for what came next in my career. Even though the company eventually sold off the department, the work I did there echoed beyond my time, and opened the door to my next opportunity. That risk, just like the one before, became a stepping-stone to growth.

Taking risks doesn't mean being careless. It means believing in your future self enough to move forward, even when the outcome isn't guaranteed. You don't need to be fearless, you just need to be ready enough.

"You won't always feel ready. Leap anyway, your wings will strengthen on the way down."

STAY CURIOUS, STAY RELEVANT

For designers and artists alike, staying curious is essential to remaining creatively alive. One of the most powerful tools you can cultivate is your openness to inspiration from outside your immediate field. I often look to fashion, architecture, interior design, and photography to spark new ideas or push the boundaries of a visual solution. Exploring other creative disciplines helps you evolve your own design voice, and makes your work more layered and unexpected.

Be intentional about seeking out new perspectives. Visit museums, explore galleries, flip through international magazines, scroll through online portfolios, or walk through unfamiliar neighborhoods. Observe what other artists, makers, and even unrelated industries are doing.

When I first started as a graphic designer, the *Communication Arts* journal quickly became my go-to source for creative inspiration. Whenever I felt uncertain about which direction to take on a new project, I'd flip through its pages and find a spark, something visual, something unexpected, that nudged me forward. Over time, the more I exposed myself to great work, the more I built up a visual vocabulary of ideas, styles, and approaches I could draw from when I needed it most.

Great designers are naturally observant. They notice details others overlook, whether it's the curve of a chair leg, the texture of a building, or the natural beauty of butterfly wing patterns. They're fascinated by both the microscopic and the cosmic. Curiosity isn't just a trait, it's a practice. You have to train your eye to look deeper, linger longer, and connect ideas across disciplines.

You never know what will inspire you until you let yourself be surprised. Keep your mind open and stay adventurous. The more you explore, the more the world gives back. What once seemed ordinary becomes extraordinary, layered with new meaning, just waiting to inform your next design.

LET GO OF WHAT YOU CAN'T CONTROL

Following on from the previous principle, here's a hard but freeing truth: you can't control everything. And the sooner you make peace with that, the more power you'll feel in your life.

When one of my jobs was eliminated, it wasn't because of anything I did. I had only been in the role for a few years, I loved the team I was part of, and I was doing great work, but corporate decisions were made, and I had no say in the outcome. The job was simply gone. I couldn't change that. The normal feelings of it being a targeted decision about me filled my mind, was it because I am a Latino? Or was it because I had been in the company a long time and was much older than the rest of the staff? I felt like I had been personally attacked. But that was not the reality, and those are normal feelings. You are human after all.

This reminded me of an even more personal lesson I learned when I was just 13 years old. I lost my younger brother in a tragic traffic accident. He was in the wrong place at the wrong time, and nothing I could do would change that. The pain of that loss has never fully gone away, but I've learned: blaming ourselves for things outside our control isn't healthy.

In life, you can control your attitude, your effort, and your values. But you can't control the weather, other people's behavior, or corporate restructures. Trying to control the uncontrollable only leads to unhealthy frustration and fear.

Instead, make a plan. Talk to the people who care about you. Prepare for what you can, and let go of the rest. Peace of mind comes not from control, but from clarity about what's yours to carry, and what's not. In the case of the eliminated job, I ended up in a much better job very soon thereafter.

EVERYTHING IS TEMPORARY

We talk about "permanent jobs," but the truth is, nothing is permanent. And that's not meant to scare you. It's meant to prepare you.

Layoffs, restructures, and unexpected changes happen every day. Early in my career, job security felt like a given. But over time, that illusion faded. We live in a fast-moving, ever-changing world. What you can do is stay sharp, stay flexible, and make yourself as essential as possible. You can't guarantee job security, but you can control how you show up.

And remember, bad leadership is temporary too. Some leaders can make your life miserable. But I've held on to one truth: this wouldn't last forever. And it didn't.

Even now, I know this next phase of my life will also end one day. That's the nature of things.

No job is forever. No feeling is either, and that's okay.

EMBRACE THE SHIFT

If you've ever worked at a forward-thinking company, or really, any company that wants to stay relevant, you know that change is constant. New structures, new leaders, new tools, new goals. Some changes are exciting, but others are uncomfortable. Change, whether welcome or not, is necessary because it is how we evolve, not just as organizations, but as individuals.

Years ago, I experienced a shift that felt more like a gut punch than a growth opportunity at the time. After two years working in my first graphic design job, my husband received a well-deserved promotion. But, the job was in California, which meant selling our home in Florida and moving our entire lives across the country. While we had visited California before, we had never considered uprooting our lives and making it our new home.

We talked through every angle. After weighing the pros and cons, we decided to take the leap and move. On the surface, it felt like an exciting opportunity, but in reality, it was far more complicated than it first appeared. We hadn't considered the logistics: selling our home in

Florida, arranging movers to transport everything we owned, including our cars; finding a new place to live in California; coordinating the transfer of my job. Thankfully, my company at the time was incredibly understanding and gave me several months to plan the transition once we were settled.

But the shift was still overwhelming. When we finally landed in California, we were hit with culture shock. Both of us had grown up in smaller cities, and now we were living in the middle of enormous Orange County. We had never driven on ten-lane highways, and we quickly learned that in California, you plan your day around traffic. We also faced the reality that we would not be able to afford buying a home because of the steep prices in that market.

The pace, the scale, the constant movement, it was all jarring. And beyond the logistics, we didn't know a single soul there. The flight response I had felt years earlier when moving to the U.S. came rushing back.

Still, amidst the disorientation, there were unexpected gifts. Over time, both of us landed job promotions, with increased pay and greater exposure. We found things in California that simply weren't available in Orlando, more cultural events, art exhibitions, and creative spaces, which I especially appreciated. And we can't forget the mountains! Slowly, we started to feel more stable. But in truth, we never felt fully at home there. It always felt temporary, like a bridge to something else, something not yet defined.

And then, a year later, another promotion gave us the opportunity to return to Florida. That decision opened more doors than we could have imagined. By that point, change no longer scared us. We had learned to adapt. And most of all, we had leaned on each other. The strength of our relationship made it possible to endure the chaos, the discomfort, and the unfamiliarity. That chapter taught us that change, while often messy and unwanted, can become the very thing that unlocks what comes next. It was certainly a rewarding experience that opened new doors for us personally and professionally.

Change doesn't always look like opportunity on the surface. Sometimes, it brings discomfort, disappointment, or even betrayal. But here's what I've learned: resisting it rarely makes it easier. What does help is adjusting your mindset. Not every change is ideal, but every change can be a teacher. If you stay adaptable, stay clear about your values, and stay focused on your own growth, you'll find a way forward, even when the path looks different than you expected.

HOLD THE VISION, EVEN IN THE FOG

Throughout my career, there were times when I felt defeated, especially after not getting a job I truly wanted or thought I deserved. It's normal to feel that way. But here's something important to remember: it's not always personal. If an employer passed on me, I reminded myself, it was their loss. I know what I bring to the table.

When I received a rejection, I gave myself a few days to sit with it before revisiting it with a clearer head. Once I felt more grounded, I used that moment to reflect: What could I improve? What might I be missing? If possible, I'd reach out to the hiring manager to ask for feedback, what was lacking in my portfolio or approach? Taking that initiative turned a "no" into a learning opportunity.

And here's the truth: you only need one "yes" to make all the "no's" worth it.

BE A STUDENT, ALWAYS

No matter how long you've been doing this, there is always something new to learn, a technique, a tool, a point of view. I am learning new tools, techniques, and trends every day. The design world evolves constantly, and so must we. Stay curious, ask questions, and seek feedback. Sit in the front row again and again, even when you've already earned your seat at the table. Mastery comes not from knowing everything, but from remaining open to everything. That's the key.

I know it can feel uncomfortable to join support groups where you don't know anyone at first. But I've learned that this kind of discomfort is often where the best growth happens. Putting yourself out there, hearing new perspectives, sharing your own, can be a powerful part of the learning journey. It helps you understand how others think, and in turn, deepens your own creative work.

If showing up in person feels intimidating, online groups can offer a similar space for connection and support. They've been a lifeline for me more than once, especially during seasons when I struggled to be outwardly social.

As an introvert, I've had to nudge myself into the spotlight, even when it didn't feel natural. I often think back to my early days in theater, being on stage, exposed and unsure, yet still showing up. Those moments taught me more than performance; they gave me the courage to be seen. And that courage has helped me introduce myself in new rooms with confidence and humanity.

LEAVE A LEGACY, NOT JUST A FILE FOLDER

Your career is more than a collection of projects, it's the impression you leave behind. The people you mentored, the standards you raised, the moments you inspired. Legacy isn't about being famous; it's about being remembered for the way you worked, led, and lifted others. Someday, the files you designed will be archived or replaced, but your influence on people will endure. Design with that in mind.

When I design, I don't think about legacy, not consciously, anyway. Since design has become part of my DNA, I know that everything I create leaves a mark. It influences, it communicates, it helps people consider something, whether it's a marketing campaign, a book cover reveal, or a full brand transformation.

But imagine this: every project, every decision, every idea you bring to life is a small stone on the road of your legacy. You're building it, moment by moment, pixel by pixel. You may not see it clearly now, but one day, someone else will walk that road and see the path you've paved.

DESIGN WITH INTEGRITY

This one should go without saying, but it still needs to be said: **don't steal**. Always design with integrity and intention. That means working with an objective mind, staying curious, and using all the elements and tools of design responsibly. These aren't just learned behaviors, they should be part of your creative DNA.

Searching for images on Google, downloading them, and inserting them into your project without a license? That's theft. The same goes for typefaces, music, photography, video, iconography, and graphics. Anything that someone else created. Just because something is online doesn't mean it's free to use.

But integrity isn't just about copyright, it's also about sensibility. I once worked with a co-worker who had dabbled in graphic design. He proudly told me about an ad he created for a bank that featured a woman with exaggerated breasts, claiming it would grab the attention from male customers. He wasn't joking. To him, this was just smart marketing. To me, it was unethical, misogynistic, and completely unprofessional.

Design has power. That power should be used with care, empathy, and thoughtfulness. When we create, we shape perception, and that comes with responsibility.

Do the right thing. Even when no one is watching.

MEET THE DEADLINE, HONOR THE CRAFT

Deadlines aren't just calendar dates, they're a test of your professionalism, time management, and respect for others' time. As creatives, we often crave more time to polish or perfect, but learning to deliver great work on time is what earns trust and opens doors.

Deadlines define how we're seen in the professional world. Miss them repeatedly, and people stop depending on you. Meet them consistently, and you become the person others can count on, even under pressure.

As I got more comfortable with my work, I could tell how long a project would take me to design in order to better plan my day, inclusive of any fires that I would have to put out or meetings I needed to attend. For me good planning helps me meet all my deadlines.

QUICK TIPS

- Break down the timeline into smaller milestones.
- Build in buffer time, life always throws surprises.
- If you can't meet a deadline, communicate early and honestly.
- Done is better than perfect.

RESPECT THE SPECS

Before you dive into any project, know your specs. Dimensions, resolution, color models, and file types aren't just technical details, they're essential tools in making your design function as beautifully as it looks.

Failing to meet specs can lead to production delays,

pixelated images, or wasted materials. Respecting the specs is part of respecting your client, your craft, and your own credibility.

DESIGNING FOR PRINT

- Dimensions: Usually in inches or feet, depending on size (posters vs. billboards).
- Color Mode: CMYK
- Resolution: 300 dpi minimum
- Common File Types: PDF (for printing), JPG, PNG
- For animation: GIF or MP4 (depending on usage)

DESIGNING FOR DIGITAL

- Dimensions: In pixels
- Color Mode: RGB
- Resolution: Standard is 72 ppi, but 150 ppi is becoming more common with higher resolution screens.
- Common File Types: JPG, PNG, GIF, BMP
- For animation: GIF or MP4

Great design isn't just about creativity, it's also about

precision. Specs are the invisible frame that holds your brilliance in place.

CREATE WHAT YOU WISHED EXISTED

I came across this phrase on Instagram one day, and it stuck with me: *"Be a voice, not an echo."* It reminds me why I design in the first place. Yes, we often work within the boundaries of budgets, brand guidelines, and client expectations, but creativity doesn't have to stop there.

As designers, we have the power to stretch those boundaries and bring something unexpected into the world. We can invent new ways of communicating visually. We can surprise, disrupt, and inspire.

An inventive designer doesn't just follow the template, they break the mold. They take calculated risks, try new things, and explore ideas that might not always work, but are worth the experiment. That's how your individual voice develops and that's how you help move design forward, not by echoing what already exists, but by imagining what could.

Don't wait for someone else to make the thing you want to see. Create it yourself.

TIME IS THE REAL CREATIVE TOOL

There's a common misconception that design is easy. If it were, the world wouldn't need designers. The truth is, it takes talent, strategy, and imagination to do what we do, and above all, it takes time. Wait! And gut too, I can't forget that!

Design isn't just decoration. It's problem-solving, storytelling, and visual communication. When time isn't factored into the process, creativity suffers, and so does the team behind it.

I've worked with teams where leadership overlooked or avoided the time needed for good design. Everything became a last-minute scramble, leading to burnout and low morale. This is not sustainable, and it's not respectful to creative professionals.

Strategic planning that includes space for creativity leads to better work and healthier environments. Designers are not production machines. We bring ideas to life. Without us, those brilliant marketing ideas remain just that, ideas. Give creatives the time they need, and they'll give you magic.

DESIGN FOR IMPACT, NOT APPLAUSE

Applause is fleeting, but meaningful design has staying power. It's easy to get caught up in chasing awards, likes, or client praise, but the real magic happens when your work connects, solves, uplifts, or educates. Impact lives in clarity, in usefulness, in how a message moves someone. When you design with intention and empathy, the recognition often follows, but even when it doesn't, you'll know you created something that mattered.

I've had work that didn't win awards but changed the way people saw a brand. I've designed pieces that were never featured in any gallery or magazine, yet sparked conversations, moved emotions, and left lasting impressions. The work I'm most proud of wasn't the flashiest or the most praised, it was the work that helped someone understand a message more clearly, that lifted a voice that had gone unheard, or that brought joy, calm, or clarity to someone's day. Design at its core is a form of service, and when you lead with that mindset, your career becomes less about validation and more about contribution. That's the kind of legacy worth building.

YOUR PORTFOLIO IS YOUR VOICE

An outstanding résumé is important, but your portfolio is your true voice. It's the most powerful tool you have to show what you can do and how you think. Depending on the kind of work you're pursuing, your portfolio needs to be focused, clear, and distinctive. The good news? Today, there are a wide range of free and paid platforms to help you build a portfolio that's both functional and visually compelling.

FREE PLATFORMS

Behance

It's easy to use and widely recognized by creatives and recruiters. Great for showcasing new work and building community, especially if you're just starting out. Even though customization is limited, it's fast and efficient.

Adobe Portfolio

It's free with an Adobe Creative Cloud subscription and integrates seamlessly with Behance. It provides clean templates, a professional look, and is easy to use.

Notion

It's a newer tool with lots of potential. Great for presenting case studies and context behind your work. Its templates are flexible and modern, but it's not ideal for visual galleries.

Google Sites

It's very simple and straightforward. A good no-frills option if you need something quick and easy. Not as visually rich but gets the job done.

PAID OPTIONS

Squarespace

My personal favorite. I've use it for both my professional portfolio and my book websites. Their templates are polished, mobile-optimized, and backed by strong customer support. Ideal for designers looking for both aesthetic control and marketing tools.

Webflow

It's highly customizable and robust, best for designers with advanced technical skills. It offers full creative control but comes with a steep learning curve.

Format

It's an affordable and elegant choice, especially good for photographers or visually driven portfolios with its clean and minimal templates.

WHAT TO INCLUDE

Your **About** or **Author** page should introduce who you are, not just what you've done. This is your chance to speak in the first person, share your story, and reflect your personality. Include a résumé if looking for work and consider adding behind-the-scenes photos of your process or workspace.

If your work spans multiple disciplines or industries, organize it in sections. This helps viewers focus on what's most relevant to them.

- A **Recent Work** section allows you to spotlight newer projects and demonstrate growth. You might also consider a **Case Studies** section if it fits your work, sharing your goals, process, challenges, and results can be an excellent way to demonstrate strategic thinking.

- A **Contact** page is a must, make it easy for people to reach you.

- If you're up for it, a **Blog** page is a great way to share your perspective, offer insights, or write updates about ongoing projects and success stories. It builds credibility and keeps your site dynamic.

- And finally, if you create designs you'd like to sell, consider launching a **Store** page with your art applied to merchandise like T-shirts, scarves, mugs, or stationery. Today's tools make it easier than ever.

KEEPING IT FRESH

Portfolios should evolve alongside your career. I like to update mine in sections rather than doing a massive overhaul, it keeps things manageable and ensures my work stays current. Be thoughtful in what you include, don't show everything, especially if it's repetitive or outdated. I like to remove older projects to show that I have clearly evolved in my work.

Your portfolio isn't just a collection of images, it's a narrative. It's how you show your voice, your creativity, and your values. Keep learning, keep evolving, and let your portfolio speak for you.

BUILD A CREATIVE DEPOSITORY

One tip I often share is to create a "mood board folder" for inspiration. Mine lives on my desktop and includes screenshots from social media, photos I take, articles, and posts that strike me visually. I turn to this folder whenever I'm stuck on a project or need a jumpstart.

I still remember being inspired by the Rio Olympics graphics. Years later, working on a completely unrelated project, those visuals popped back into my mind. I used them as a starting point for a new design direction. A colleague asked me how I even remembered something that specific, and I told him it's like having a file cabinet in my brain.

Now, with tools like Instagram collections or saved folders, I save anything that sparks a feeling. You never know when that memory might return with new meaning.

FEEDBACK IS A GIFT, NOT A THREAT

Yes, I've mentioned feedback earlier in the book, but it deserves to be repeated as an important design principle, as the first reminder to keep tucked in your back pocket at all times.

Feedback is not a personal attack. It's not an insult. It's not a judgment of your worth.

It's a gift, one that will shape you into a stronger, sharper, and more thoughtful designer.

I used to struggle with this. Like many creatives, I poured my heart into my work. When someone offered critique, it felt like they were criticizing me. But over time, I learned to detach emotionally, not from the work itself, but from the delivery of the feedback. That's the key.

Not all feedback will be delivered perfectly. Sometimes it's rushed. Sometimes it's blunt. Sometimes it lacks the tact you wish it had. But your job is to look past the words and find the truth inside. What is the essence of what they're saying? What can you learn from it?

Be grateful when you work with people who care enough to offer thoughtful, constructive feedback, especially those who know how to give it with respect. And if you're not getting feedback? Ask for it. That's how you grow.

Don't fear feedback. Seek it. It's one of the fastest, most honest ways to become a better designer, and a better communicator.

TRUST IS EARNED PIXEL BY PIXEL

Trust is one of the most valuable currencies you'll ever build in your career, and it's earned gradually, moment by moment, pixel by pixel.

It starts with showing up. With consistency. With delivering what you say you will. It's reinforced every time you meet a deadline, listen carefully, collaborate with integrity, and treat others with respect.

Over time, trust becomes a network you can lean on, especially when life throws you curve balls. I've been through major transitions, tough career changes, and personal losses. What made those moments survivable was the trust I had built with my peers, mentors, and collaborators. I didn't have to ask for support, it came naturally, because the trust was already there.

But trust isn't just something you build for your own benefit; it's something you pass on. Check in with people. Stay connected to your colleagues, even if you don't work together anymore. A message, a smile, or a simple "How are you doing?" can carry more weight than you realize.

Everyone's carrying something. Be the person they can count on and who shows up, again and again.

DROP THE EGO, KEEP THE EXCELLENCE

Hopefully, you'll never have to work with a graphic design diva, but chances are, you might. And honestly, it might not be the worst experience. Why? Because exposure to ego-driven designers can teach you exactly how not to be.

A "design diva" is someone who puts aesthetic over function, thinks they know better than their clients, dominates conversations with stories about themselves, and lets ego and perfectionism run the show. They often resist feedback, ignore collaboration, and see compromise as a creative failure. These traits can make them incredibly difficult to work with.

To avoid being labeled one, prioritize communication over control. Love your ideas, but don't become ruled by them. Feedback is not a personal attack, it's a tool. Treat it as a gift that helps you grow and refine your work. The truth is, you're not the only one in the room. Design is a collaborative effort, and the best results come from openness, curiosity, and flexibility.

Being humble doesn't mean being timid, it means

being wise enough to listen, curious enough to explore alternatives, and confident enough to adapt. Design trends change, tools evolve, clients bring different perspectives, and you should evolve with them.

Let your work shine through your dedication, your adaptability, and your ability to collaborate, not your ego. That's how you keep the excellence.

MAKE CONNECTIONS, NOT JUST CONTACTS

Networking is a powerful tool in a designer's toolkit, not just for uncovering job opportunities, but for discovering inspiration, mentors, collaborators, and lifelong allies. The best connections often begin with curiosity, not career ambition. Ask people about their creative journey, the challenges they've faced, and what fuels their work. Be genuine in your interest. Share your own work with confidence, but stay humble. Leave your ego at the door.

If you're meeting in person, always carry a digital

version of your portfolio that's easy to access. When you show your work, don't just hope for oohs and aahs, walk them through your process. Talk about the problem you were solving, the thinking behind your choices, and how you arrived at the solution. This builds credibility and shows maturity in your creative thinking.

And don't forget the follow-up. After connecting with someone, send a thank you message or text. They've taken time to meet you and share insights you might not find anywhere else. That small gesture goes a long way.

Attend networking events when you can. AIGA mixers, design meetups, and annual conferences like Adobe MAX are excellent for meeting others in the creative community. If you can't make it in person, look for virtual opportunities through LinkedIn events or online panels. There's always a way to engage, just take the first step.

LinkedIn, in particular, is an invaluable tool for growing your network. But it's not just about collecting contacts, it's about building real relationships. When I first joined LinkedIn, I barely knew anyone in the design field. But as I started working, I connected with colleagues and mentors I respected.

Be proactive. After you land a job, send connection invites to your team and leaders. Stay in touch with messages or shared posts. Building relationships takes time and intention.

It's perfectly okay to reach out to people you haven't met if they work in the field you want to grow in. Send a short, respectful note explaining that you're new to the industry, eager to learn, and would love to connect. Stay humble, be positive, and let your excitement for the work come through. That energy is contagious.

Be realistic, not everyone will respond. I was once introduced via email by a close work colleague to an art director from another department that he knew quite well. I took the time to respond to both, thanking my colleague for the connection and telling the art director that I was interested in speaking with him about his role. He never responded, not even after I followed up a second time. That doesn't speak much for his brand and the department he represented. I already knew they had a bad reputation so this confirmed it.

LinkedIn is also a great application to share your voice. Use it to write thoughtful posts about your design work, lessons you've learned, or articles that inspire you.

I often use LinkedIn to share updates about my books or repost stories that deserve more attention. I also write articles about things I am very passionate about, or career news. Over time, these habits naturally attract others who share your passion. It won't happen the next day, but in time you'll see the benefits.

As you build your network, remember: don't act desperate, don't only talk about yourself, and never speak badly about other designers or clients. You never know who knows whom. Networking isn't a one-time effort, it's a lifelong investment. Nurture it, feed it, and let it grow alongside your career.

LIFT AS YOU CLIMB

There is no greater satisfaction than sharing your talent and lessons learned in life with others. During my career, I have had the opportunity to mentor work colleagues and college students starting their own creative journeys. This experience reinforced my own knowledge of design, it offered others fresh insight and inspiration, and it helped expand their professional network directly and indirectly. Personally, it fulfilled the mission of my personal brand to have a positive professional reputation while building a legacy for my work that others can look up to after I am gone.

Sign up for your local AIGA or check in with employer's resource groups since many also support mentorship programs. Mentoring doesn't have to be a long-term process, it also means helping your work colleagues when they need your advice or need someone to listen to their challenges. I assumed the role many times when through my relationship building, people saw in me someone they could trust and that they could learn from. I certainly didn't have all the answers, so I did the research if it was something I could also learn from. For me, mentoring is a way of paying it forward. I was a mentee once, and while it felt like therapy at times, it was incredibly eye opening to learn how my attitude and thought process affected the decisions I made every day. There was a lot of soul searching throughout this period and I felt like a different person coming out of the experience. Rewarding others with the same experience doesn't only help you feel good but also helps keep the industry strong by raising the standard of design thinking and professionalism.

GIVE BACK WHERE YOU CAN

One of the most rewarding things you can do as a designer is to give your time and talent to those who need it most. Volunteering your skills, whether it's designing for a nonprofit, helping a small community organization, mentoring an emerging artist, or serving as a judge for an art competition, has the power to create real impact. It doesn't just elevate others; it also deepens your own growth and passion for the work you do.

When you share what you've learned, you not only lift someone else up, you reinforce your own purpose. Helping someone build their first portfolio or offering feedback on their work can be a game-changing moment in their career, and a humbling reminder of where you once started.

Give generously when you can. The design world becomes stronger, more human, and more hopeful because of it. For me, giving back started as a natural extension of my role. When my employer was looking for someone to help create the visual direction for the Hispanic Heritage Month, the employee resource group leader who knew me from previous work I had helped with, reached out to ask if I would be interested in creating the visual identity for the campaign. What began as an internal project turned into something much more significant. Designing the brand vision for such a meaningful celebration not only elevated the quality and authenticity of our message, it also gave me greater visibility as an artist and deepened my connection to my own cultural roots. It reminded me that some of the most rewarding opportunities to grow, personally and professionally, can come from simply offering your creativity in service of something larger than yourself.

IT'S A WORKPLACE, NOT A PLAYGROUND

I've always been a friendly person at work. I enjoy connecting with others, building rapport, and creating a positive atmosphere. And while work can be a place where great friendships are born, it's important to remember this: you were hired to do a job, not to make friends.

Some people come to work strictly to work, and that's okay. Everyone brings their own background, personality, and boundaries to the workplace. Not everyone will be interested in bonding beyond the day-to-day responsibilities, and that has nothing to do with you personally.

Over the course of my career, I've made some incredible friends, people I still talk to and admire. But I've also had moments where I reached out to keep a connection going, and the other person simply wasn't interested. That used to bother me. Now, I see it for what it is: not rejection, just reality.

Being professional means knowing how to read the room. Be kind, respectful, and collaborative. But don't take it personally if your warmth isn't always met with enthusiasm. The workplace isn't a social playground, it's a shared space for purpose and performance.

If friendships form, that's a beautiful bonus. If not, it doesn't make the experience any less meaningful. Focus on doing your best work and treating others with integrity, that's what lasts.

DON'T BE AN ASSHOLE

A so-called "manager" I once had the misfortune of working for told me I smiled too much, and that people thought I was too nice. It was a laughable comment, coming from someone who only respected those who kissed up to him. He didn't seem to notice, or care, that almost no one liked him. But he had the title, and in his mind, that gave him permission to treat people however he pleased. He believed that to succeed, you had to be cold, aggressive, and calculating, just like him.

I told him I smiled because I genuinely loved my work and enjoyed collaborating with people. And yes, I smiled at him too, because I could see how miserable he truly was inside. Unsurprisingly, he was eventually shown the door. But the damage these types of people cause often extends far beyond their tenure.

And the leaders who tolerate or enable this kind of behavior? They're just as guilty. If you look the other way while your people suffer, you're not leading, you're an enabler of the negative behavior. That makes you an asshole as well.

You've heard the saying, "You catch more flies with honey than with vinegar." That's not just a cliché, it's a truth I've seen proven time and time again. Unfortunately, kindness is often mistaken for weakness. And yes, confident people can come off as arrogant or distant. But it's entirely possible to be both confident and kind. In fact, those are the people others want to work with.

So don't be an asshole. Lead with empathy. Treat people with respect, regardless of titles or hierarchy. You never know, your employee could someday become your boss. Kindness is not a liability, it's one of your greatest creative and professional strengths.

OUTLAST THE SMALL-MINDED

As I've touched on earlier in this book, this point is worth repeating, because it's critical for your self-respect and long-term growth: Never let toxic leaders, or anyone else, define how you feel about yourself or your work.

It's demoralizing to work under someone who belittles others just to elevate themselves. Unfortunately, during my career, I encountered leaders like this, people who were in higher positions but had no real understanding of how to lead. They thought they could use me or toss me around simply because they had the title. But I never stooped to their level.

I showed up with professionalism, integrity, and confidence. I didn't let them make me feel small. I reminded myself every day: I was not the problem.

Here's how I survived, and thrived:

- I documented everything. Even when it took up an hour of my day, I kept a record of every interaction that crossed the line. You will need this documentation if it ever becomes an HR issue.

- I built a support system outside my team. I leaned on a company-paid therapist to talk through the emotional toll and get perspective.
- I focused on excellence. I put my head down and did the best work I could, consistently. I made sure there was no room for doubt about my performance.
- When it was clear the situation wasn't going to change, I made a plan to move on with my dignity intact and never look back.

Toxic leaders often see high-performing people as threats. They'll find any excuse to get rid of you, but that says more about them than it ever will about you. Being exposed to these kinds of people was painful, but it also taught me wisdom I wouldn't have gained otherwise.

And I'll never forget this lesson: People don't leave jobs, they leave their leaders.

So, here's what I want you to remember: Not every leader is a mentor. Some are obstacles. But their inability to lead with kindness, empathy, or integrity is their flaw, not yours. Don't shrink to fit their vision. Rise to build your own. The right people will recognize your value, even if it takes time to find them.

KEEP YOUR RÉSUMÉ SHARP AND READY

Your résumé is more than just a formality, it's a living document that reflects your evolution as a creative professional. Just like your portfolio, it should always be up to date, streamlined, and aligned with your current goals.

Length: Keep it to one page. Clarity and focus are key.

Purpose: It should instantly communicate who you are and why you're right for the role.

For designers, layout matters. Your résumé should reflect your aesthetic sensibility, clean, readable, and visually appealing. But don't get so creative that it becomes unreadable by applicant tracking systems (ATS). Many design-heavy résumés get filtered out before a human ever sees them.

Here's what to include:

- **Header:** Name, city and state, phone number, email address, and website/portfolio links.

- **Professional Title:** Directly under your name, list the role you're applying for. This helps résumé scanners flag your relevance.
- **Core Competencies:** A snapshot of your key strengths, tailor this section to each job using language borrowed from the job description.
- **Professional Experience:** List each role with:
  - Company name and location
  - Job title, and dates (month/year)
  - Bullet points with key achievements. Where possible, include results: improved workflows, successful campaigns, or growth metrics.
- **Education & Professional Development:** Include your highest degree, year earned, and any relevant training, certifications, or courses.
- **Languages & Honors (if applicable):** Include only if relevant to the position.

Pro Tip: If you're invited to an interview, bring a printed version of a more creative résumé layout. It's your chance to showcase your design chops in a way that stands out on paper. If you're early in your career or transitioning roles, highlight class projects, freelance gigs, passion projects, or even volunteer work. They reflect initiative, talent, and drive, qualities every employer values.

OWN YOUR INDEPENDENCE

As in many types of work, freelancing is a great way to make extra cash and even grow your own business if you so desire. Throughout my career, I had the opportunity to work on projects externally in addition to my day job. This allowed me the opportunity to have some creative freedom by working on different brands and styles, while also making some extra cash. It also helped me experiment by trying new tools and techniques I had never used before.

By freelancing, I was also able to work on my own schedule, this is especially an intelligent choice for anyone looking to build a business of their own. You can build a better work-life balance that way.

At first, it was difficult to engage and even get freelance

prospects. I simply reached out to my small network and asked them to pass the word to their networks as well. Now there are many online options to choose from where you can advertise your independent availability. Once you have built a more experienced resume, you'll see that freelancing jobs will come your way much easily. Because of my experience in credit union branding and design, I have had the ability to produce work for a variety of banking institutions.

One more thing I love about freelancing is that you get to choose who you want to work with and how much to charge for your work based on the amount of work, complexity of the projects, and hours it would take to do the work.

Freelancing is not for everyone though. There were times at the end of a hard day of work that I didn't feel like clicking on a mouse for another 4 hours. Because design work takes so much brain creative power, it was a struggle for me at times to manage the amount of work. I didn't like saying no to anyone that reached out because I was worried that I would later lose other future opportunities. Remember your health and work-life balance is more important. But if you have no choice because you are looking for that additional income, consider limiting the number of hours each day you put into the freelance work. Instead of promising work the next day, give yourself more time in order to spread out that work into smaller time increments.

For freelancers that do this as their full-time job, collaborating with other creatives and sharing projects with them would also allow you time to build your own network and business.

AFTERWORD -
THE PIXEL DUST
I FOUND

When I first joined the workforce, I never imagined the journey would take me to where I am today. I didn't expect graphic design to save me, or to bring me such lasting joy and purpose. Since I was a child, I loved art very deeply, but the world around me made that dream of working in that field feel out of reach. Family expectations, cultural norms, and my own self-doubt clouded the path ahead. Making a living as an artist felt unrealistic, even naive. I didn't have mentors or role models to show me what was possible, and for a long time, I felt lost, adrift in the uncertainty of what a future could look like without a clear direction. I spent years chasing belonging, hoping to find purpose in any creative role that would have me. Naturally, animation pulled me in first. Though I never received the screen credit I longed for, that world opened my eyes to the power of visual storytelling.

Those early jobs, even the ones that felt like detours, guided me, step by step, toward graphic design. And when I found it, something clicked. It felt like home. I wasn't just creating, I was communicating, influencing, and solving. I was building something meaningful. Slowly, I carved a space for myself. My work began to stand out. I found fulfillment not just in the craft, but in the impact it could have. Of course, it wasn't all magic. I experienced rejection, financial struggle, and professional abuse. I've worked under people who tried to break me down simply because they thought they could. But from those hardships, I learned about resilience, about dignity, and about the kind of leader I never wanted to be. I also learned the value of those who did believe in me, those who gave me a chance not because I knew someone, but because they saw what I had to offer. I owe them more than they know.

In those early days, I lived paycheck to paycheck, surviving on credit cards and sheer determination. I never wanted fame, I just wanted to be a good artist. Someone who contributed to the profession. Someone who helped move design forward. That passion never wavered. With time, effort, and heart, I matured from learner to leader, from hopeful outsider to respected creative. Animation taught me to honor the power of detail. Design taught me how to speak through images. Both gave me the tools to evolve.

I remember being asked during my 30th work anniversary celebration what I believed had sustained my long career. The answer was simple: become the best at what you do. Love what you do. And while everyone is technically replaceable; talent, experience, and integrity make you indispensable. But above all, it's about showing up, with professionalism, humility, and a good heart. That's how you build a career and leave a legacy.

And maybe that's what finding pixel dust really means. It's not just about magic in the fairy tale sense, it's about uncovering something rare and meaningful in the everyday work we do. It's in the quiet moments of growth, in the projects that push us, in the relationships that shape us, and in the resilience we build when no one is watching. Pixel dust isn't handed to you; you find it when you show up again and again, heart open, hands ready. I didn't find it all at once. I found it pixel by pixel, over years of trying, failing, learning, and daring to keep going. And if you're on your way, I know you will find yours too.

FOR THE DREAMERS

I hope this book has done more than simply share my story, I hope it has lit a spark within you. Maybe it's the seed of a dream you once tucked away, believing it was out of reach. Maybe it's a reminder that your creative voice matters, even if the world hasn't heard it yet. Wherever you are in your journey, just starting out, making a shift, or reigniting a long-dormant passion, I want you to know that it's never too late to begin again.

If you've ever held back because you didn't believe in yourself, or because the resources weren't there, know that you're not alone. I've walked that road. And still, through persistence, support, and self-discovery, I found my way. I never gave up. My hope is that these pages encourage you to trust your instincts, invest in your talent, and take the next step, however big or small, toward the creative life you envision.

Whether your path is brief or boundless, I wish you clarity, courage, and joy. May your journey bring you not only success, but also fulfillment, purpose, and pride in the legacy you're building, one project, one dream, one pixel at a time.

ACKNOWLEDGMENTS

As I've said earlier in the book, no one can do it alone in the world. I have a lot of people to thank and those listed here are just a few of them that have supported and believed in me even when I doubted myself. Thank you for crossing paths in this thing we call life. In alphabetical order: Raul Adames, Albano Humberto Aguilar-Anderson, Mariela Aragon, Annette Arauz, Ileann Barsallo, Roger Barton, Sarah Berry, Olga Bravo, David Bufler, Scott Burkhardt, Steve Burkhart, Ace Carreon, Irma Cartaya, Raul Cisneros, John Cole, Nitza Correia, Anarkelly Cosca, Brian Crimmins, Isaac Crop, John Davis, Luis de la Espriella, Danielle DiMartino, Andrew Downin, Trevor Dreher, Janet Dunham, Marc Easter, Jeff Ebershohl, Alex Eiserloh, Francisco Flores, Raquel Gabuya, Colleen Gay, Renée Elise Goldsberry, Sergio Guillén, Emily Hand, Judy Haner, Kate Hartig, Shawn Hooper, Samantha Hubbard, Joelle and Brian Hutchins, Connie Jackson, Matthew Jones, Melia Keller, Ralph Kent, Amy Keys, Quynh Kimball, Eric Klee, Mouguett and Jose Lozada, Alex Maher, Monty Maldovan, Kamilah Marshall, Kathy Massee, Lisa Montgomery, Christopher Moore, Sean Moore, Zenia and Tommy Morris, Corey Moseley, Scott Myles, Leigh Nelson, Wilfredo Nuñez, Dawn Ockstadt, Jean-Paul Orpiñas, Sonia Ortiz, Chris Parker, Thomas Patti, Rick Pearce, James Peshek, Sandra Porter, Sammia Pratt, Bruce Quinn, Genevieve Rodriguez, Mark Rodriguez, Angel Sarria, Jan Sileo, David Silva, Roberto Singh, Karen Sitz, Amy Skiff, Ye Su, Peter Theo, Brad Tichenor, Teo Trandafir, Juliana Trujillo, Mario Urquia, Gegham Vardanyan, Noelia Villareal, Steve Vollmer, Tony West, Shellie West-Postal, Mia Winters, Nilena Zisopulos, and Darren Zwein.

ABOUT THE AUTHOR

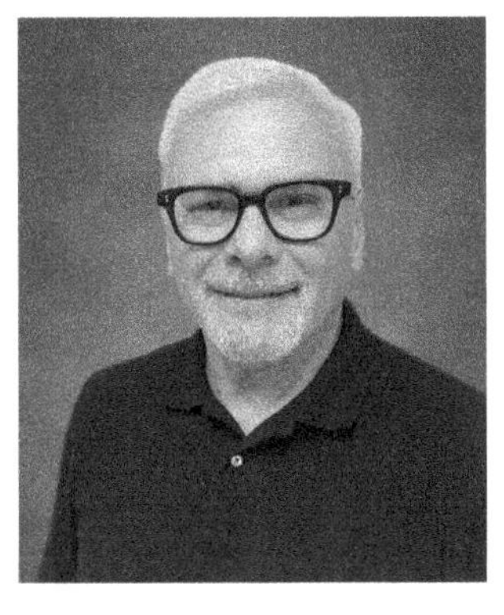

E.H. DE LA ESPRIELLA is an award-winning designer, author, and creative leader with a 30-year Disney career that spans animation, branding, publishing, and beyond. He built a dynamic career in graphic design, leading creative direction in publishing, sports, and financial services.

A passionate storyteller and fine artist, his mediums range from oil painting and collage to photography and writing. His first book, *Sun Night*, a creative nonfiction reflection on childhood and loss during his youth in Panama, received national recognition. E.H. shares the lessons of a life in design through *Finding Pixel Dust*, a deeply personal, visually inspired guide that explores creativity, resilience, and the power of finding your place in the world, one pixel at a time.

Learn more at delaespriella.com/books

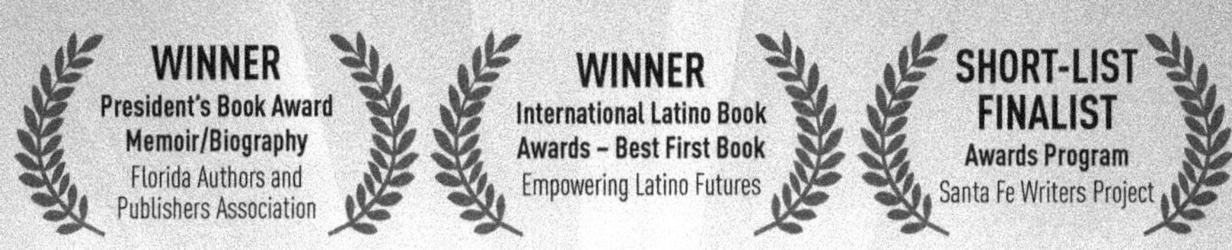

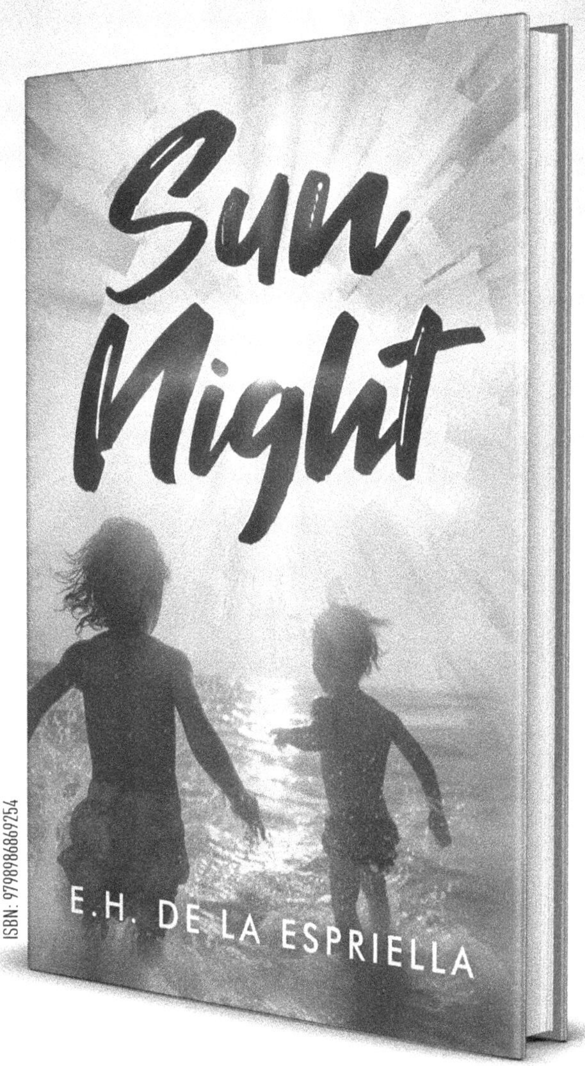

"This book is magnificent, unique, and well executed. It felt like I was hearing the story around a campfire. E.H. de la Espriella as an author, has impeccable instincts when it comes to the craft of writing."
—Andrew Gifford, author of
We All Scream: The Fall of the Gifford's Ice Cream Empire

Visit delaespriella.com/books for details • Available wherever books are sold